Suburbia:
Civic Denial

A PORTRAIT IN URBAN CIVILIZATION

Suburbia:
Civic Denial

By *Robert Goldston*

Illustrated by Donald Carrick

The Macmillan Company

The Macmillan Company
866 Third Avenue, New York, New York 10022

Collier-Macmillan Canada, Ltd., Toronto, Ontario

Library of Congress Catalog Card Number: 76–99120

First Printing

MAP BY JACK FULLER

Thanks are due to the following for permission to include
copyrighted selections:

George M. Cohan Music Publishing Co., Inc., for "Forty-
five Minutes from Broadway" by George M. Cohan, Copyright by George M. Cohan Music Publishing Co., Inc.

Harper & Row, Publishers, for "Commuter" from *The
Lady Is Cold* by E. B. White, Copyright 1925 by E. B.
White. Originally appeared in *The New Yorker*. Reprinted
by permission of the Publisher.

J. B. Lippincott Co. for "To the Little House" from
Chimneysmoke by Christopher Morley, Copyright 1921,
renewal 1949 by Christopher Morley.

6692

Contents

Suburbia:
Civic Denial

New Rochelle—
only forty-five minutes from where?

In Search
of Suburbia

Heaven is not built of country seats,
But little queer suburban streets.
                    —CHRISTOPHER MORLEY

Which would seem to indicate that a vast section of
America is laid out on the divine plan. Spreading for .
miles in all suitable directions from every American
city, large or small, are infinite webs of "little queer
suburban streets." But these streets, however queer,
are not all the same. Some of them run through old,
established areas of graceful and highly expensive
mansions; others checkerboard dreary wastelands of
tiny, clapboard dwellings, alike to each other as cof-
fins. And between these extremes may be found suburban areas displaying every variety of design,
planning and income level. Some suburbs are so
densely populated as to be indistinguishable from the
residential sections of their neighboring cities; others

are so thinly settled as to verge on true countryside. Some, because they have engulfed older small towns, may boast a civic nucleus or center; some pretend that the local school-*cum*-P.T.A. is a civic center; many make no pretensions to civicism at all. As for the people who live in suburbia—they are called suburbanites, exurbanites, or the even uglier descriptive-accusative "megalopolitans." They, along with their environment, are regarded with the deepest suspicions by sociologists, anthropologists and psychologists, with horror by urbanists and intellectuals, with loathing by artists. And suburbia is considered somewhat less than celestial even by those who inhabit it. Yet it is the environment of many millions of Americans. If present trends continue, it may soon include fully half the population of the United States.

The word "suburban" has a pejorative connotation even in its literal definition. It means "beneath-urban" or "less-than-urban," that is, a civic environment which is less highly organized, less developed than that of either a city or a town. Thus, to start out with, suburbia is at once defined not in positive but in negative terms. Other definitions are not much more useful. Some observers claim that suburbia is that area inhabited by suburbanites—and then proceed to define suburbanites as those who depend upon a neighboring city for their source of income, either as commuters directly working in the metropolis or as local "service" people catering to such commuters. But because definition by source of income is at best hazy (what of local dairy farmers who depend on city markets?), some observers add an arbitrary distinction, based on density of population, between city-dependent rural people and city-dependent suburbanites. Some urbanists define suburbia as that area which has no civic nucleus, no civic center of government but is administered rather by county or state officials. This definition, however, would exclude many a self-governing small town which is clearly, both through proximity and economic dependency, a suburb of some larger nearby city. Some of the most acute observers define suburbia largely as a state of mind—and in many ways this most subjective definition is the most objectively useful.

The extension of cities and their combining with adjacent wasteland to form megalopolis further complicates the search for suburbia. This includes not only great cities (such as New York and Boston) but also smaller cities (Newark, New Jersey, Hartford, Connecticut, and so on), small towns, clearly visible suburban areas *and* that vast, undefined, haphazard development of roadside catering and housing which has blotched so much of the American landscape. Megalopolis already exists on the eastern seaboard of the United States, stretching from Boston to Washington; it is rapidly developing on the West Coast between Los Angeles and San Francisco; it threatens to fill in the countryside hubbed on Chicago as far north as Milwaukee, as far east as Gary, Indiana, and west into the infinity of the Great Plains. It is thus the overall environment within which suburbia increasingly exists and it therefore has a direct impact on suburban life. It is profitless to imagine suburbia as the built-up countryside around a city which in turn evaporates into farmland or true rurality. Suburbia today does not evaporate—it links other suburbs in a complex

chain or grid pattern with other distant cities. Farmland is slowly but surely excluded from megalopolis;
rurality is to be found only in parkland (national or
state) or in undeveloped wasteland. Because megalopolis truly exists only on the Eastern seaboard, and
because it prefigures, apparently, what will soon exist
throughout the country, our search for suburbia will
be centered within the megalopolitan environment.

Suburbia in all its varied forms, once considered a
reasonable or regrettable complement to city life, is
today increasingly looked upon as the outright enemy
of urban culture. It is from the suburbs that millions
of automobiles pour into America's cities every day to
choke their streets with traffic and their inhabitants
with noxious smog. It is from suburbia that the huge
throughways, expressways, parkways, and highways
knife into the hearts of the cities to turn the urban
landscape into a nightmare of concrete swaths. It is
from the suburbs that millions of commuters pour
daily into the city to take advantage of its economic
opportunities, its tax-supported services, thereby im-
posing a heavier and heavier burden on taxpaying city
dwellers. It is to the suburbs that middle-class city
dwellers, the solid core of the city's prosperity, civic
consciousness and political stability, have fled. Suburbia in relation to the city has been likened to a
cancerous growth. As more and more suburban "cells"
come into being, they coalesce, still feeding upon the
city which is their center. As they coalesce, they grow
in economic and political power, thereby becoming
able to demand of state, regional and national authorities more and better means of exploiting the city

while continuing to avoid the tax burdens of city life. And as the city decays under this assault, more and more of its "better" citizens move away from it—to suburbia, leaving the city a sort of central commercial-industrial slum from which suburbanites may make their living, but to which they contribute nothing. Eventually the city dies, of course.

This view, while useful, is an oversimplification. No American cities have yet died, nor do they show any signs of impending mortality. On the other hand, it depends what one means by a "city." If it is defined simply as a small area with a very high density of population and a large number of inhabitants drawn together because the city is the most efficient tool for the exploitation of a particular environment (and this is the average American view), then the permanence of our cities cannot be questioned at present. But if by city one means a place primarily devoted (whether consciously or not) to the heightening of human experience and awareness through the multiplication of human contacts and the intensification of every human expression—economic, cultural, artistic and political— then America's cities are in an advanced stage of moribundity.

But this fact cannot be blamed solely upon the growth of suburbia. Rather this growth, insofar as it has proved an undesirable and antihuman response to the American environment, is simply itself a symptom of that same basic civic disease which afflicts American cities; which, in making them uninhabitable, spurs the growth of a suburbia which, in turn, makes them more uninhabitable still. And this disease, which may be labeled "lack of civic concern," is itself deeply rooted in the American way of life, the national experience.

Economists and other professional fretters about the national well-being pinpoint the "decay of the public sector" of the economy as opposed to the private sector. By this they mean that the national income is devoted far too much to private satisfaction rather than public well-being. This is especially notable in American cities. TV antennas mushroom like forests from the roofs of decaying slum buildings; expensively glossy cars jam inadequate and poorly maintained streets; millions of dollars are poured into cultural centers for the higher arts while the public school systems decline. The examples may be endlessly multiplied. Yet the American way of life, uniquely based on the national experience of settling and exploiting an almost uninhabited continent, is devoted to the private exploitation of any environment for private profit. Private support of the public welfare, whether direct or indirect (administered through the government) has traditionally been enlisted only when the decay of the public sector can be demonstrated to threaten private well-being or prosperity. For example, on the national level, federal aid to education became politically feasible only when Russian achievements in space technology seemed to threaten America's technological superiority, upon which, in turn, the national security rested. Only when individual citizens could be persuaded that the decay of public education might eventually result in the destruction of their private worlds would they support the massive taxes necessary to begin to remedy a national disgrace. On a

Megalopolis disposes of its refuse by pumping it into the sky

local level, only when smog had made the air of New York City positively dangerous and began killing citizens could political support be enlisted for the passing of antipollution laws. The adequate *enforcement* of these laws will, no doubt, not become politically feasible until thousands of private citizens die of smog inhalation.

This devotion to private rather than public welfare is partially, but not fully, responsible for the rise of suburbia. It is, however, absolutely responsible for the fact that suburbia has become a civic cancer destroying the vitals of American cities—just as it is the root cause for those cities decaying without the help of suburbia.

The essential lure of suburbia may thus be described as a desire to return to childhood, to withdraw from a threatening, increasingly complicated, increasingly remote, apparently unrewarding public arena to a private nest not unreminiscent of the womb (in Florida and California there are suburban houses whose architecture is alarmingly womblike). And as we shall see, suburban life has other, more reasonable attractions. But the symbiosis of suburbia and its metropolis and (in the case of the Eastern seaboard) its megalopolitan matrix is now so intricate and so enmeshed in a "vicious" circle of problems that it may be much more rewarding to investigate what positive life-styles can be gleaned from suburbia than simply to denounce the whole phenomenon.

The rise of suburbia (which in turn was one of the vital factors in the rise of megalopolis) has been one of the major causes of the decay of American cities (and also foreign cities from London to Leningrad, from Sydney to Tokyo). But it has not been the only cause. In any event, it is not reasonable to expect people to return to blighted urban centers no matter what the cause of the blight. Suburbia-megalopolis is not only the civic framework within which more and more Americans try to devise a personal and a public life-style; it is also here to stay, at least for the foreseeable future. City planning, civic improvement movements, attempts to regenerate American public life which do not take this fact into account are totally unrealistic. Attempts by urban centers to make war on suburban-created problems (by extending the city-tax area, for example, or by cutting the main highway arteries into the city as a means of dealing with traffic strangulation) are also doomed to defeat until suburbia itself has been reshaped.

But the existence of suburbia, and perhaps even of megalopolis, the central problem of American civic life today, is also a challenge and, most important of all, an exciting opportunity to find new answers to urban problems. The fact of the problem suggests not only its own solution but also a large part of the solution of some of America's deepest metropolitan problems.

Meanwhile it would be well to take a look at suburbia and its megalopolitan matrix with as few preconceptions as possible; and to understand what it is today, we had best begin with its history. For suburbia does have a history—a surprisingly long one. . . .

1 The Rise of Suburbia

The manner of most gentlemen and noblemen also is to
house themselves (if they possibly may) in the suburbs
of the city, because most commonly, the air being there
somewhat at large, the place is healthy, and through the
distance from the body of the town, the noise is not
much; and so consequently quiet.

—JOHN STOW

Mr. Stow, an eminent Elizabethan, was writing at the
beginning of the seventeenth century, and the city to
which he had reference was London. If it is found
surprising that his words might be perfectly well applied to any modern metropolis, it may be found
enlightening that they could also be applied to ancient
Babylon, and even to Ur of the Chaldees. For suburbia is no modern phenomenon: it is as old as the
very idea of a city, which is to say, as old as civilization
itself.

Archaeological research has uncovered, for example,
a "Greater Ur" of suburban villas and streets that
stretch four miles from the walls of that Biblical city.
Egyptian funerary models and paintings often show

us suburban houses with spacious gardens. Greek cities, such as Athens and Sparta, were surrounded by developed space—buildings, gymnasiums and villas, and gardens which can only be described as suburban. The suburbs of ancient Rome have left traces still visible today. Yet despite this wealth of evidence, it is widely assumed that suburbia is a recent development. Its existence is explained by (or blamed on) the Industrial Revolution, which, by making cities all but uninhabitable, supposedly drove those lucky or rich enough to escape out of the city and into the surrounding countryside. This was, no doubt, an essential factor in the creation of modern suburbs—but there are other factors, one of which is far more important and pregnant with disaster. In any event, it is not suburbia which is new—only certain suburbs.

Originally any suburb was simply the area beyond but close to the city's defensive wall. It was differentiated from open countryside by the fact that it was inhabited by or used by people whose lives and work centered on the city, not the country. It was an area where urban institutions requiring space could be conveniently developed. Outside most ancient Greek cities could be found a gymnasium and an academy—both needing large spatial areas which could not be found within the city's constricting wall and both depending for their existence on city, not farm, dwellers. It was not shepherds who attended the Athenian academy, but the sons of wealthy Athenians. Those who worked at the academy might maintain a small house and garden nearby (as did the philosopher Epicurus), but such places were looked upon as "retreats" from city life, not substitutes for it.

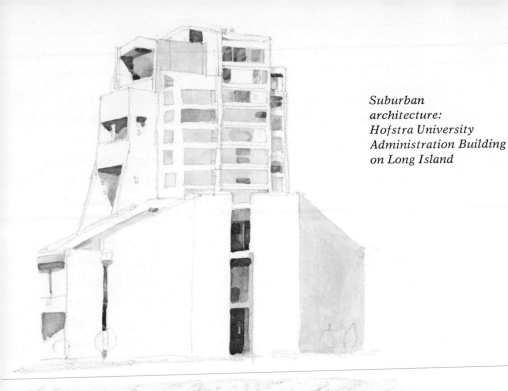

*Suburban
architecture:
Hofstra University
Administration Building
on Long Island*

In the ancient world, political and military uncertainty made it extremely risky for anyone to establish their principal dwelling (with all their household goods) beyond the fortification offered by the city wall. It was only when a more widespread military-police security could be offered by advanced political organization that city dwellers could feel free to center their lives beyond the wall. Thus the most extensive suburban development in the ancient world was undoubtedly that surrounding Rome. Rich Romans felt free to live beyond their city's walls because peace and order were guaranteed not so much by masonry as by the efficiency of the legions; when that efficiency collapsed, Roman suburbia disappeared.

Roman and Greek development of suburbs was repeated in medieval times. As civic life reemerged from the wreckage of the ancient empires, and as the incursions of invading nomadic tribes gradually ceased, both institutions and people ventured forth from the protective city walls. After the twelfth century, monasteries were often built outside city walls (before that time they were almost always built within them), where they could better fulfill their needs for more ample space and seclusion. Universities such as Oxford and Cambridge which, although they had grown up within the walls of smaller towns, depended for their existence on the city of London, began to expand beyond the fortifications of their respective towns. And alongside institutional expansion beyond the city, once again (as in the earlier, more secure Roman world) went an invasion of the nearby countryside by the rich. At first, as in ancient Greece, the villas and cottages of medieval merchants and master craftsmen were summer retreats; but by the sixteenth century, with public order more or less guaranteed by national armies and administrations, they were no longer secondary "vacation" structures, but the principal homes of their occupants. Instead of commuting occasionally to the countryside suburb, those who could afford it commuted from the suburb to the city.

Both in ancient and medieval times, one of the principal factors in driving individuals to seek residence beyond the city itself was the fear of disease. The physicians of the ancient world of whom we have any record were constantly advising people to seek the fresh air and healthy atmosphere of the countryside both to avoid city-bred infections and as a sovereign "cure" for almost any malady. From the thirteenth century on the dread of bubonic plague caused periodic mass migrations from cities. The characters in Boccaccio's *Decameron* were wealthy refugees from an epidemic of plague that was sweeping their native city, Florence. They escaped to nearby Fiesole, which was already a well-developed suburb. Likewise, wealthy Parisians fled to the "Left Bank," and wealthy Londoners to the open suburban landscape between the City and the city of Westminster when plague descended. As Lewis Mumford has pointed out, the modern suburb may be said to have begun as a sort of rural isolation ward.

But it was not only the negative factor of fear that lured city dwellers to the suburbs, even in medieval times; there were also positive aesthetic and psychological reasons. Although the older, historic cores of such cities as London, Paris, Barcelona and Florence may have seemed as graceful, beautifully proportioned and humane to their medieval inhabitants as they do to us today, nevertheless, no matter how attractive any surroundings may be, the human eye and mind demand variety. Medieval and Renaissance cities, even after their walls were torn down, were still organized to make the most efficient use of a relatively small area. The more closely packed the streets, houses and plazas of an old city, the greater was the visual relief of the open suburban landscape. On the other hand, a constant and unchangeable diet of country landscape could prove as eye-tiring and mind-dulling as its opposite. The ideal solution, on an aesthetic level, was to be sought in the daily shuttling to and fro between countryside and city.

On the psychological level, the early suburb offered unparalleled opportunities for personal expression. There, beyond the restrictions of urban confines and civic architectural codes, individuals could build whatever struck their fancy. Country houses built as miniature castles and monasteries, set in parks where hedges had been trimmed into the shapes of fantastic beasts, were not uncommon as early as the seventeenth century. Architects felt free to experiment as boldly as they wished because their buildings were isolated by large expanses of greenery and because they had only to satisfy the personal whims of a single family. Later, during the nineteenth century, suburban houses aped Chinese pagodas, Arabian mosques, railroad stations, Greek temples—any kind of structure at all. It has been reserved for our own time to build suburban houses (especially in southern California and Florida) which pretend to be hamburgers, camels, ships and insects.

The point to be made here is not the increasing grotesqueness of suburban architecture, but the continuing impulse toward freedom and fantasy which can be traced from medieval times to the present day. The freedom sought was of a very personal nature. Leone Battista Alberti, an Italian architect writing at the end of the fifteenth century, stated: "There is a vast satisfaction in a convenient retreat near the town, where a man is at liberty to do just what he pleases . . . I, for my part, am not for having a [house] in a place . . . [where] I must never venture to appear at my door without being completely dressed." In other words, over three and a half centuries ago Alberti was enraptured with the informality of suburban life, and

American townscape—Red Bank, New Jersey

expressing one of its cherished defenses as clearly as it could be stated today.

Of course, for centuries this escape into fantasy was reserved only for the very rich. It was only they who could afford to build suburban houses in the first place, only they who could afford to maintain the coach and horses necessary for daily commuting to work (and, it may be added, only they who could afford to come to their offices late and leave early). In fact, it is hard to distinguish, during the seventeenth and eighteenth centuries, between true "country houses," as the seats of the English aristocracy were called, and suburban houses. Perhaps the only useful difference was that the suburban houses were close to London. The seepage of suburban life through the class structure of society over the centuries followed the rising standard of living and the mechanization of life.

Thus, at first, as in London and Paris, it was the titled aristocracy who, wishing to escape the plagues and noisome filth of the cities yet remain close to the royal court, established suburban houses (many of them as ample as palaces) in the open land just beyond the old city walls. They were followed later by the rich merchants, bankers and shippers who, if untitled, still from 1700 onward commanded the necessary wealth and leisure to lead suburban lives. During the nineteenth century middle-class shopkeepers, retired army and navy officers, the more prosperous tradespeople and even such as factory foremen and chief clerks began moving into suburbia. In our own day it has been only the poorest classes of society who cannot afford this escape.

Just as industrialization tended (over the long run) to raise private incomes to what may be described as "escape level," so too it lowered escape costs. Cheap mass public transportation was offered first by the railroads and, on the fringes of some cities such as London and New York, by the development of subways and trolleys. Inexpensive private transportation in the form of the motorcar and the publicly financed highway followed. And the industrialization of the housing industry, leading up to today's prefabrication methods, combined with the sophistication of new means of financing, brought some sort of suburban dwelling within the price range of all but the poorest people.

The earlier railroad suburb had several distinct advantages—advantages which are clearly seen now only after they have almost disappeared. First of all, these suburbs were discontinuous. They perforce grew around towns on the main railroad routes—and train stations were never closer than three miles apart, usually more than five miles apart. Furthermore commuters, lacking motor transport (anyone who has ever attempted the care and feeding and managing of a horse will realize that horse and buggy transportation is in no way similar to auto transport), could not establish themselves too far from the train station. So between railroad suburbs green belts of natural countryside or cultivated farmland remained. This not only preserved the country matrix around the suburban town, it also was a natural compressor of early suburban growth—a certain density of population and development was assured that is by restrictions of space based on restrictions of local transportation.

Another advantage of the railroad suburb was that

since it depended on main line railroad stations and since these had already been built at small towns, suburban development was centered around a pre-existing civic nucleus. Although suburban commuters might work in the nearby city, they lived in and around a recognizable and functioning civic core complete with a town government, local political complications, a town hall and, of course, a town shopping area, generally clustered around the railroad station. There was, in other words, a pre-existing pattern of civic life into which the new suburbanites could fit. So long as most suburban houses had to be "within walking distance of the depot" (as real-estate agents and builders always advertised), the invasion of suburbanites never threatened seriously to disrupt or "swamp" local towns and their civic patterns. On the contrary, a *naturally restricted* influx of ex-city people generally brought increased prosperity to established communities as well as such benefits as better schools and medical services.

Another type of older suburb was the preplanned "garden suburb." During the last decade of the nineteenth and the first few decades of the twentieth centuries, land speculators and real-estate men, correctly judging the potentialities of suburban growth, would buy up choice land on the outskirts of a large city, hire architects and planners and create from scratch a new community of homes. Once again, as long as the railroad offered the only means of rapid transit to the city, these new communities had to be within easy reach of a station. But sometimes the railroads were persuaded to build new stations. From the planning viewpoint,

and architecturally, the garden suburbs (such as River-side near Chicago, Roland Park outside Baltimore, Llewellyn Park in New Jersey, Bronxville in New York) derived from the much earlier concept of a country house set in a gardened park. The planners and architects of garden suburbs created a new form of urban rationalization. They did away with the small city block and for it substituted the new suburban superblock, an area many times as large. Within this superblock housing density averaged about twelve houses per block, thus maintaining a balance between rural isolation and city crowding. Because preplanning on this larger scale did away with the need for so much roadbuilding, and showed great economies in the construction of sewage systems and so forth, money was available for gardening the entire area—making it into a consciously created park. Furthermore, unlike most city planners, the suburban planners followed the natural contours and eccentricities of the land instead of steamrolling it flat, thus preserving natural variety in the landscape.

In concept and design it is very hard to fault the older garden suburbs. But they did lack one element which railroad suburbs built up around small towns had: a civic core and hence meaningful civic life. It was to remedy this lack that the community center concept was first developed. The idea of a building which, in the absence of a town hall, would serve as a place for neighbors to gather to discuss and act on local problems gained much support during the twenties and thirties of the present century. Community centers (generally built near local schools) sprouted and flourished all over suburbia. They benefited from the fact that in the preplanned garden suburbs an older element of American life, which had been all but destroyed in the cities, came back into being—neighborliness. So long as suburbs were restricted in population and area they developed into real neighborhoods, places where most people knew each other and participated in the common social and political local life as equals. For a brief period of time, in fact, many observers of suburban life hopefully detected in it many of the same elements that had brought greatness to the life of the ancient Greek cities such as Athens. Here were small, homogeneous communities of relatively well-off people with good educations (or at least better than average educations) whose men to a certain extent and women to a large extent had the leisure necessary to devote themselves to civic affairs. Furthermore, the suburbs had an advantage Athens lacked —the slave class upon which this well-being and leisure depended did not live in the community; it was quartered in the slums of the nearby city.

Unfortunately, Athens was not re-created in pre-World War II America. In fact the very idea that anyone could realistically have expected such a development seems ridiculous today. Suburbia has become synonymous with complete disregard for civic affairs; it has even come to stand for the abolition of the whole idea of "neighborhood." When one thinks of suburbia today, one does not think of small towns nestled around railroad stations, or of gardened parks; one thinks of endless miles of dreary and dilapidated box houses undefined in any civic or even social way.

The physical reasons for this are fairly apparent. The introduction of the private motorcar and its eventual adoration as the supreme "good" in life may be cited. The population explosion may be mentioned as well as the increasing decay and befoulment of cities and the burgeoning of cheap means of construction. All of these have led to an explosion of suburbia which in itself has defeated the original ends of suburban development.

With the coming of the motorcar, the pedestrian scale of suburbs disappeared. They ceased to be neighborhood units and lost whatever individuality or charm they may originally have possessed. The motorcar was an invitation to increasing isolation. Profit-hungry real-estate speculators could now build developments anywhere at all, unrestricted by the need for rational public transportation. Every man in his car was an atomized unit. Just as he could live anywhere to which a road could be built, so he could shop anywhere, play anywhere and send his children to school anywhere—the limits being drawn only by convenient driving time. And driving time was to be made more and more convenient by the introduction of faster cars and, above all, by the building of highways, parkways, expressways and throughways. That these huge lava-flows of concrete ate up so much of the suburban landscape as to render it hideous (consider the suburbs of Los Angeles or Long Island outside New York City) made no difference. That the introduction of high-speed traffic into so much of the suburban countryside tended to isolate suburban communities one from another at the same time that it tended to turn those communities into formless sprawls of housing was equally unimportant. Protests against the new superhighways and their supercars came not from the sub-

urbs which they ruined, but from the city, now threatened with traffic strangulation.

The motorcar conquered space privately (as the railroad and air transport conquered it publicly). And as
space was conquered, the number of people to whom
it was accessible was drastically increased. From being
the preserve of the rich, suburbia became the refuge
of all but the very poor. And modes of construction
were developed to satisfy all economic levels, employ-
ing ever shabbier materials, ever more meager designs.
Simultaneously suburban densities were increased so
that plots of land small enough for the most restricted
purse could be provided—thereby effectively eliminating personal privacy.

But it is not in these physical developments that the
reasons for the destruction of the original suburban
dream is most profitably found. The real reasons were
always part of the dream itself. What, after all, impelled people to leave cities in the first place? It must
be remembered here that we are not talking of those
who desire to live in the country—either in a small
country town or on a farm—but of people who do not
want to remove themselves from the urban environment, only to improve it by broadening it to include
the nearby countryside. Suburbanites are suburbanites
precisely because they desire to be near enough to the
city to enjoy its benefits, but not near enough to have
to shoulder its burdens.

The ruthless industrial-commercial exploitation of
cities which has been going on now for more than a
century, with all the evils it has brought—in the fester-
ing of huge and rotten slums, the increase in urban
crime and violence, the corruption of urban politics,

Red Bank Airport—flight to where?

the befoulment of the urban environment, the nerve-straining and mind-numbing tensions of urban life—all of this is *not* a necessary or inevitable part of urbanity itself, but rather a corruption of it. That this corruption has led to urban disaster in our own day no one would deny. But faced with disaster, there are two, not just one, possible responses—either to do something about it or to flee.

And, as we have seen, the essential impulse behind the development of suburbs has always been flight—flight from the plague, flight from overcrowding, flight from visual monotony—and now, flight from poisoned environments. The basic idea of retiring into one's own house, at a distance from neighbors, and living a life closer to one's inner fantasies is so deeply personal a decision as to escape broad-scale social analysis. But when this idea grips millions of people, then it becomes an observable and criticizable social phenomenon. The now typical suburban life, family centered, wife administered, devoted above all to the goals of consumption and play, is in its *social* aspect today a regression from civic responsibility. Suburbia is thus both a symptom of deep civic disorder and a contributing factor to continued civic disintegration. But is this inevitable in the very idea of suburbia? No—not necessarily. Are there no aspects of suburban life which might not provide clues to the regeneration of the cities? There are many. But before we can bring them to light, it might be well to take a look at some representative suburbs as they are.

2 Where the City Used to End: Yonkers

Only forty-five minutes from Broadway,
Think of the changes it brings;
For the short time it takes, what a difference it makes
In the ways of people and things.

—GEORGE M. COHAN

In that more luxurious but now remote era before the First World War, those forty-five minutes, spent in the plush-upholstered commuter cars of the New York Central, the Pennsylvania or the Hartford–New Haven Railroads were sufficient to translate city-weary New Yorkers into a wholly different environment. Leaving the "cares" of the city behind, early twentieth-century suburbanites were treated to a trip through open farming countryside before they reached such independent and "uncontaminated" country towns as Yonkers, New York—our prime example of a former "railroad suburb." Today, after half a century of "progress" in transportation, the commuter cars are plastic-upholstered, the journey takes just as long by train—and it takes considerably longer by automobiles jammed bumper-to-bumper during rush hours. But in any case there is little reason now to make the trip. Yonkers has been all but devoured by its colossal neighboring metropolis—only a change in the color of the street signs indicates where New York City ends and Yonkers begins.

Not that the transition is necessarily unpleasant. Commuters riding the New York Central trains that leave the heart of Manhattan (at Grand Central Station) have only to bury their faces in newspapers, close their eyes or concentrate on a game of bridge to avoid seeing the filth and squalor of Harlem and parts of the lower Bronx as they rush by to happier climes. And once the trains reach the upper Bronx and the Hudson's eastern shore, commuters are treated to a splendid view of the New Jersey cliffs dreaming across the polluted river. Commuters driving their own cars up the Henry Hudson and Saw Mill River parkways could well imagine they were surrounded by nothing more than "garden city" and "green belt" developments, so well insulated are these routes (but of course in return for this insulation, commuting motorists must bear the frustration of trying to park or garage their cars in New York City; they must have nerves of iron to face monumental traffic jams; they must display fatalistic courage in the face of steadily mounting accident statistics).

Once they reach Yonkers commuters are in many senses (certainly in the legal sense) outside New York City; but in many ways they are not. They are in an independently self-governing community with its own civic nucleus which is officially described as a

"city." Indeed, it is the fifth largest city in New York State and in many a foreign country or western state would be considered a large urban complex. Yet insofar as a huge proportion of its population is employed in New York City and uses Yonkers mainly as a nursery and dormitory, the city is a suburb of New York. More than that—the feverish development of the decades since World War II has all but made it into a neighborhood of New York. Its present condition and its development are fairly typical of an entire class of suburbs throughout the United States (from San Pedro, outside Los Angeles, to Evanston, outside Chicago, to Lynn, outside Boston)—small towns that grew into cities precisely because of their proximity to large metropolises, and have now been reduced to suburban neighborhoods of their expanding, neighboring giants.

The history of Yonkers began in 1639 when the Dutch West India Company (whose claim to New Netherlands, the present New York State, was based on the explorations of Henry Hudson) bought land along the Hudson River above their settlement at Nieuw Amsterdam from the Keskeskeck Indians. Title to the area passed from the Dutch West India Company to the New England Company in 1646 when the English seized New Netherlands—and in that same year the land comprising most of present-day Yonkers was sold to one Adriaen van der Donck.

In the tradition of Dutch New World settlement, Van der Donck made himself "lord of the manor," rul-

Yonkers City Hall—tiny oasis and disappearing memory of civic independence

ing his broad acres in semifeudal style and trying to lure farmers and craftsmen to his huge private estate. Part of the lure was Van der Donck's construction of a saw mill at the juncture of the Hudson River and a much smaller stream, the Nepperhan. The Nepperhan still flows through Yonkers, but most visitors and more than a few citizens would be hard put to find it. The farmers and trappers who settled on Van der Donck's land considered him slightly "uppity" (the very idea of attempting to set up a semifeudal domain in the rugged New World wilderness was something less than realistic), and referred to him sarcastically as "de Jonkheer" (the young lord). It is from the corrupt pronunciation of that phrase that the present name Yonkers derives.

But Van der Donck was not the last romantically inclined young lord to attempt the importation of European modes to New York. In 1672 Frederick Philipse bought most of the Van der Donck land and, in turn, constructed his own manor house in 1682. In 1779 the third and last Philipse "lord of the manor" lost his lands and his house because of his essentially unrealistic view of the world—he supported the British during the American Revolution. The Philipse manor house was preserved (a beautiful example of colonial architecture, as a public museum it now houses a priceless collection of Gilbert Stuart paintings) but the Philipse land was parceled out and sold to local farmers and settlers.

For the first half of the nineteenth century Yonkers remained little more than a place name; one of those dreamy little Hudson River hamlets familiar to Washington Irving when he wrote his "Legend of Sleepy

Hollow." The farmers of the area sold their produce to wholesalers in distant New York (twenty-five miles south, a full day's horseback ride, more than a day's cart-haul) and watched paddle-wheel steamboats and barges pass down the Hudson from Albany to "the city." Few of them could have realized that this river traffic spelled the end of their semi-isolation. For with the opening of the Erie Canal in 1825, linking the Hudson with the Great Lakes, New York City became the prime port not only of New York State but of the entire American Middle West. And as it did so, it began to expand in the only direction open to it—north along the Hudson. As New York came closer, the Yonkers farmers found it increasingly easier and more profitable to sell their produce to the city folk—and the city folk began to settle in this nearby, prosperous area. Land values rose, the old river road linking Yonkers and New York was improved and farmers were increasingly tempted to sell off some of their acreage for fat profits. By 1855 no less than 7,500 people resided in Yonkers—and on April 12 of that year they officially incorporated themselves as a village.

Partly because of lower land prices and tax rates than those prevalent in New York City, partly because Yonkers' several miles of Hudson River waterfront afforded berthing for ocean-going vessels at considerably lower costs than the already overcrowded New York City docks, partly because the Hudson continued to provide low-cost transportation to the interior, and partly because the newly expanding railroads took the water-level route of the Hudson's eastern shore to Albany and then west, industry began moving into the village even before the Civil War. What was to be-

Yonkers' Hudson riverfront today;
exploitation triumphant

come the world's largest manufacturer of elevators and escalators opened there in 1854; one of the world's largest producers of liquid sugar for industrial purposes followed shortly thereafter. And the new industries attracted not only workers from the surrounding countryside but also a heavy influx of workers from New York City. By 1872 the population of the village had almost tripled to 20,000, and on June 1 of that year it was chartered as a city by the State of New York. Growth in the succeeding century kept pace with two factors—sudden spurts of industrialization (during World Wars I and II) and, since about 1910, a dramatic increase in the number of commuters. Today Yonkers boasts about 225,000 residents.

It is thus apparently fair to say that Yonkers owes its status as city to the proximity of New York City. Its industries are there largely because of the nearness of New York City facilities and its labor supply market: those elements which make Yonkers self-sustaining and independent are thus originally dependent upon the metropolis. In this sense Yonkers may be regarded as a *haphazard* "satellite city," at least until recent times. On the other hand, examining the Yonkers population statistics more closely, it is discovered that of the 225,000 residents, only about 32,000 are employed in *local* industry. If Yonkers population statistics follow the national pattern, this means that *more than half* the working population is employed elsewhere—namely, New York City. In other words, as an independent satellite city, Yonkers can at present support a population of about 110,000; the other 115,000 use it as a suburb of New York. This civic schizophrenia brings both blessings and curses.

Following a national, and as we have seen in the preceding chapter, an historical pattern, *suburbanites* in Yonkers enjoy a higher income than average. Their income brings the Yonkers average up to about $11,000 per family—well above the national average of about $7,700 and well above the New York State average of about $9,000. This means an artificially high tax base for the city, which in turn reduces the tax burden on people who work *in* Yonkers. Real estate taxes (the largest single source of civic income) have been increasing over the years, but today average a low $60 per $1,000 assessed value (low in comparison with New York City for commercial and industrial property, low in comparison with more *purely suburban* areas for residential property).

But if the presence of suburbanites in Yonkers provides a lower tax base for those who work as well as live there, that presence also makes demands on tax income and puts a strain on the metabolism of the city. For example, there are no less than 29 elementary and 11 junior and senior high schools in Yonkers, with a total enrollment of nearly 30,000 pupils. Using national averages again, the true population of Yonkers should provide no more than about 12,000 pupils. On the other hand, the very presence of those additional 18,000 students, as well as making demands on the physical school structure, also makes a demand on the quality and level of education provided. Thus Yonkers boasts more than 1,400 teachers—slightly less than one teacher per 20 pupils, which compares very favorably with New York City and even more favorably with small cities which are not also suburbs. The reason seems apparent—suburbanites, with higher

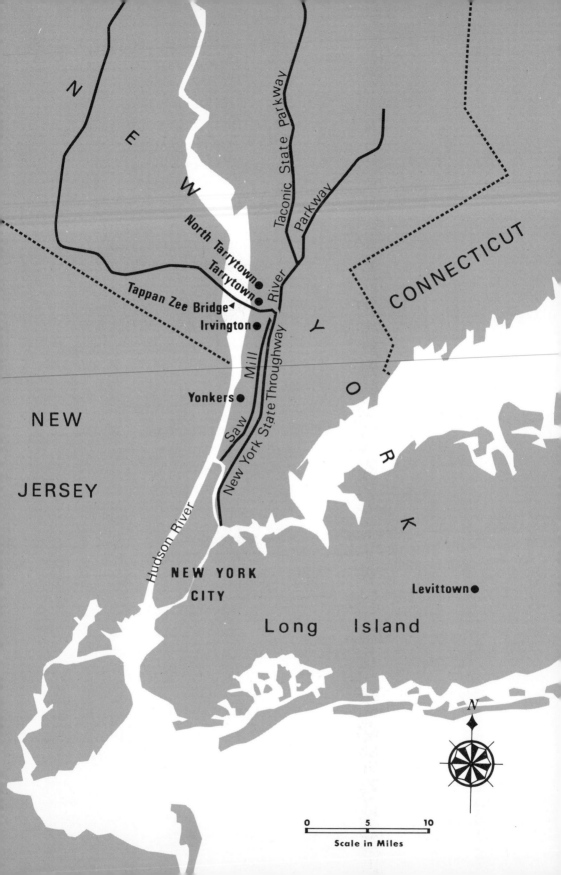

than average incomes, the social and cultural background of a metropolis behind them, the entire suburban emphasis on child-rearing stimulating them, demand a better than average education for their children. In this way children of Yonkers citizens who are not suburbanites benefit directly from the suburbanite invasion.

This basic dichotomy of increased strain (and increased taxes) but better service runs through all of the Yonkers metabolism. Thus there are no less than twenty fire companies in Yonkers—widely scattered and requiring more per capita mobile equipment because of the suburban housing sprawl; yet able to control fires so that loss per capita hovers around $2.50— a very low fire-loss rate which benefits all citizens through lower insurance rates. And again, this city with a proper population of about 110,000 must support a police force equipped for more than double that number of citizens—more than 500 men and women, including an intelligence unit (!) and a tactical squad (presumably for riot control). But, while it is never safe to ascribe causes to statistics, the size of Yonkers' police establishment may have something to do with the relatively low crime rate in the city. Likewise Yonkers, according to life insurance actuarial tables, enjoys better health than New York City—and, more to the point, better health than such nonsuburban cities as Schenectady and Syracuse in New York State—probably because of its higher per capita income and resultant higher per capita investment in health facilities. There are no less than six hospitals in Yonkers, providing about 1,200 beds—a very high ratio to the population.

The split in Yonkers between its indigenous working population and its suburban dormitory population even extends to the city government. Yonkers is governed by a mayor (elected citywide) and twelve councilmen elected one each from the city's twelve wards for terms of two years. Presumably all power is thus vested in the city's Common Council and its mayor. But in 1940—precisely, according to population statistics, when Yonkers' suburban population had reached a full 30 per cent of overall population—a city manager was appointed. Today Yonkers continues to have a city manager (he is chief executive and administrative officer of the city). The city manager form of city government, because of its increased efficiency and honesty, might well appeal to nonsuburban as well as to suburban residents. But it is hard not to suspect that, all questions of honesty and efficiency aside, the introduction of a city manager represented also an attempt on the part of the newly powerful suburban element to "have their own man at City Hall." The city manager, that is, probably represented at first a suburbanite "end run" around the entrenched indigenous city political machine. Whatever the city manager may have represented originally, there is little doubt that the entire city has benefited from the institution of the office.

What do the people in Yonkers do? Those who work there work overwhelmingly either in manufacturing or in retail trade. More than 15,000 are employed by local factories, and another 11,000 are employed in retail trade! This proportion, way out of line with national averages, is itself a clue to the structure of the city. Almost as many people are employed selling things to suburbanite residents as are employed in basic local industry. Furthermore, there are no less than 6,000 people employed in service industries—another measure of how heavily Yonkers depends on its suburbanite population for its income.

These facts of Yonkers' metabolism, with their obvious clues to the split personality of the place, are reflected as in an enlarging mirror by the physical layout and appearance of the city. Seen from the Sawmill River Parkway (named after Van der Donck's mill) or the New York State Throughway, the built-up downtown area of Yonkers, misted by the smog of New York City (which reaches miles farther north up the Hudson Valley) and nestled on gently rolling hills above the river, is not unattractive. Piercing the smog for closer examination, however, leads to disillusionment. It is then seen that the graceful spire of City Hall (and its pleasant surrounding parklet) which dominates the Yonkers skyline is no more than a relic of vanished gentility. The central city, composed largely of decaying five- or seven-story brick buildings, now is dominated by several huge square concrete monolithic office buildings. Large areas are devoted to parking space, even larger areas to factories and warehouses. Yonkers streets (which are, mercifully, *not* laid out on the armed-camp grid pattern of most American cities) are congested by traffic far beyond that which they were designed to support—another suburbanite contribution. The older buildings, built originally of red brick, are black and grimy; the newer buildings, built of gray concrete, will soon be as dirty beneath the all-pervasive smog of New York.

The Yonkers waterfront, which stretches for about

*Yonkers, hovering
between expansion and decay*

four miles along one of the world's most naturally beautiful rivers, is given over entirely to industry. In fact, only in certain small areas can anyone legally reach the riverfront or walk along its banks. And if the terrible pollution of the Hudson is primarily the fault of neighboring New York, Yonkers' riverfront industries contribute their share, too. When one considers the humane possibilities of the Yonkers environment—the hills, the mighty river, the excellent views of the Jersey bluffs beyond—one contemplates the riverfront warehouses, factories, oil and gas storage facilities with a sense of outrage. A decayed and rotting ferry pier (no longer used) gives no more than a wistful hint of what the riverfront might have been, to what human rather than exploitive uses it might have been put.

The physical impression of central Yonkers—decay, exploitation of the environment, disregard for human values—is a faithful reflection in turn of the city's social problems, which on a smaller scale, encompass most of the social problems of nearby New York. Here again one encounters the black ghetto, a jumble of rotten tenements trapped in the downtown area; the appallingly high crime rate of the central city; the replacement of juvenile violence by increasing drug addiction; the snarl of urban racial tensions which reaches into the schools. In other words, all the woes, or most of them, from which suburbanite New Yorkers have fled have followed them to this suburban city with the result that the 50 per cent of the Yonkers population which live in the city as a suburb of New York live as suburbanites in relation to Yonkers as well.

Residential communities within the city limits with names like Colonial Heights, Bryn Mawr and Strathmore house a prosperous, socially isolated population which may be classified as suburban to New York and sub-suburban to Yonkers itself. The difference between the housing accommodations, the quality of public works (street pavement, sewers, landscaping) and the quality of life in central Yonkers and Yonkers' sub-suburban communities is as glaring as the difference between life in a New York City slum and life in a country club. But what of the benefits supposedly conferred on Yonkers by its suburbanite population— the improved schools, the better medical facilities, the lower taxes combined with higher average incomes, the increased police and fire protection, and so on? It is apparent that these benefits exist *only insofar as they are necessary to the comfort and well-being of the suburbanite population.* It is painfully obvious that they have had but little impact or effect upon the central city where nonsuburbanites work and live.

Why, after all, does the 50 per cent of Yonkers' population which earns its living in New York City prefer to house itself in Yonkers? Obviously, to provide a better personal and family environment for life than that afforded by the New York urban jungle. This, in the face of what New York City has become, is, on a personal level, a completely understandable and even laudable motive—simple self-preservation would seem to dictate such a move. But the obverse side to that particular response to urban disaster is, as we have seen, as old as the history of suburbia itself—flight from civic problems rather than a struggle to resolve them. It would not, then, be realistic to expect people who have fled from one civic catastrophe to come to grips with another, even on a much smaller scale.

But it must not be supposed that suburbanites are responsible for the urban decay of Yonkers or the rape of its natural environment. There is nothing in the city's history or its socioeconomic structure to indicate that its native nonsuburban population has ever looked upon it as more than a place to exploit for private gain—a civic outlook which Yonkerites share with almost all other Americans. It did not require the suburbanite invasion to convert Yonkers' naturally beautiful waterfront into an industrial slum and refuse-heap; that was accomplished long ago. Nor did suburbanites inflict central city decay and ghetto tenements upon Yonkers; these also are native to the place. It can only be said that the conversion of Yonkers from independent city to suburban city, with its accompanying growth of sub-suburbia around Yonkers, has in no way mitigated or helped to resolve the city's basic problems.

The life of suburban New Yorkers as sub-suburban to Yonkers follows the same pattern to be found in areas purely suburban to New York itself. Sub-suburban Yonkerites are served by branches of central city stores (less and less shopping is done in the central city); highway and road construction to the sub-suburban communities consumes a heavy proportion of Yonkers' taxes while central city streets remain a mass of potholes; sub-suburban schools are modern and attractive while central city schools resemble something out of a Dickensian nightmare; more and more vital central city space is consumed by parking

lots to accommodate sub-suburban dependence on private cars while the central city's public transportation system is overburdened and irrational; the fragmentation of social nuclei away from the center follows the sprouting of large shopping centers increasingly distant from the city itself. In other words, if Yonkers (to a large extent) represents the results of the phenomenon of civic disintegration within New York City, that same disintegrative process has begun in Yonkers itself.

Such is Yonkers—not untypical of the "first wave" of railroad suburbs which proliferated on the fringes of American cities from 1900 to 1939. But Yonkers (or San Pedro, or Evanston) is not what most Americans think of when the word "suburb" is uttered. So before examining some of the possible solutions to the problems of the older railroad suburbs, it might be well to take a look at other, perhaps more familiar, suburban examples.

3 Where the Country Used to Be: Levittown

A universal suburb is almost as much of a nightmare,
humanly speaking, as a universal megalopolis: yet it
is towards this proliferating nonentity that our present
random or misdirected urban growth has been
steadily tending.

—LEWIS MUMFORD

"Proliferating nonentity" is the key phrase—that contagious spread of groups of residential areas with no civic identity, no civic form (not even an inherited one), no discernible civic-social purpose. The disease produces, most obviously on the surface, a rash of small housing units, all identical (or almost so), all set upon plots of land smaller than the area of a medium-sized city apartment. The symptoms, however, vary with the income level of the people to whom the disease is offered.

Painfully familiar to everyone who has ever driven out of an American city is the most common form of this suburban rash: the huddle of clapboard houses, mostly prefabricated, all identical one with the other,

set in rigid rows of rectangular streets like an old Roman Legion camp. Local realtors do not attempt to disguise the shoddy construction materials employed or the barrenness of the setting or the closet-sized room layouts of the houses. Instead they concentrate on displaying almost fully automated kitchens, congested with "free" refrigerators, washing machines, dryers, and so forth. All of which shine and hum but represent only a tiny fraction of the true cost of the house, however shoddily constructed. Such suburban developments rarely pretend (with the exception of their inevitably Olde English names) to be more than they are—namely, brutal real estate speculations intended to turn a quick and large profit by providing barracks-type housing in a prison-farm setting for lower-income groups fleeing the high rents, congestion and social violence of the cities but unable to afford the extravagantly high cost of home building or buying. These cardboard-box housing developments are much in evidence. They may be said to represent the most painful form of the disease of civic disintegration, but this is certainly not the fault of the *suburban idea* in itself, any more than big city slums may be attributed to the *idea* of urbanity.

At the other extreme of suburban development (and, of course, much less in evidence) are those areas in which large (but not farm-size) plots of land are offered for sale on which the buyer is to build his own house. The real-estate development in this case limits itself to landscaping, the provision of roads, sewers, and so forth—and the maintenance of high enough land prices combined with strict enough zoning to ensure the absence of overcrowding and commercial exploitation. Fairly high building standards are often maintained in such developments, the prospective land purchaser being forced to construct a house of certain proportions and in certain materials to conform with the standards of other dwellings in the development. So spacious, parklike and ample are some of these developments that they may be mistaken for natural countryside dotted with expensive houses. Only (in an increasing number of cases) the guardhouse, electronic fencing and police dogs at the entrance may indicate that the visitor is entering a preplanned social *unit*—and only the fact that the males of this area commute daily to the nearby big city may characterize this unit as "suburban." Those enclaves of the well-to-do may be said to represent the least painful but also least common form of civic disintegration—but, again, they are not the result of the suburban idea in itself any more than the exclusive penthouse apartments of Manhattan are a necessary concomitant of urbanity in itself.

To get a balanced picture of suburban development it would seem best to concentrate on neither extreme (both of which have much more to do with economics than with civic or anticivic choices) but to examine a suburb self-consciously and intentionally based neither on want nor whim, but rather on classic suburban assumptions—Levittown, Long Island.

Slightly more than twenty years ago, the approximately twenty square miles of Levittown were devoted almost exclusively to potato farming. But real-estate speculators and builders Abraham Levitt and his son William saw a more profitable crop potential on the treeless Long Island plains. Buying out the potato farmers, in 1947 they constructed five hundred Cape Cod-style houses. These were offered for rent at $65 per month—with an option to buy for $6,990 ($58 per month and *no down payment*). Thousands of World War II veterans, caught in the postwar housing shortage, rushed to rent or buy. In 1949 the Levitts added ranch-style houses which, like the Cape Cods, boasted four rooms and an expansion attic. The ranch-style houses (no more Cape Cods were built after 1949) sold for $9,500 each.

The Levitts were able to maintain these low prices by the application of prefabrication and mass-production techniques to the building industry. At one time they were actually completing 150 houses per day. Not only did the Levitts profit from their building techniques (they are estimated to have made about $5,000,000 profit from the venture), but their investment was largely secured by the United States Government—through its guarantee of World War II veterans' mortgages under the G.I. Bill of Rights—and almost all the buyers were veterans. Today Levittown comprises about 22,000 houses and its population hovers near 90,000. The Levitts have long since gone on to manufacture other instant suburbias in other states, while their methods have been copied throughout the United States. Behind them they have left a community against which it may be instructive to test certain assumptions and clichés regarding suburban life.

First of all, it has been widely assumed that the "flight" into suburbia is a flight away from political participation in the overly complex, seemingly hopeless tangle of urban problems. At a superficial glance Levittown would seem to support this view. The area itself is unincorporated—it falls within the jurisdiction of the townships of Hempstead and Oyster Bay. Furthermore, in the sprawl of Levittown, many house-owners are actually legal residents of the surrounding towns of Hicksville, Wantagh or Westbury. Apparently, for those living in the unincorporated area, political expression is limited to voting for officials of Hempstead or Oyster Bay—much older communities whose problems are not exclusively or even primarily those of Levittown itself.

Yet these appearances are deceiving. Levittown supports a flourishing gaggle of civic groups devoted to such ends as better schools, maintenance of a public library, Community Chest drives, and so on. A surprisingly high proportion of Levittown residents devote time, energy and even money to these civic organizations. Coming into a structureless civic vacuum, Levittowners very soon learned that they would have to form civic associations to handle all sorts of problems. In large cities (specifically New York in this case), the political participation of citizens in that which most immediately and closely concerns them—their neighborhood affairs—had long since evaporated, replaced by a complex structure of citywide government which did not even recognize the existence of neighborhoods. Politics in the big city had long since become the affair of professional politicians and urban experts. But in the new suburbs, as in Levittown, residents found themselves forced to undertake a "do-it-yourself" program of civic action. Thus personal political participation in civic affairs, far from evaporating in the suburbs, has experienced a rebirth precisely because (and insofar as) the suburb remains a comprehensible neighborhood-sized unit.

Another assumption that may be tested against the Levittown experience is that suburbanites tend to huddle together in ethnic ghettos and, even more, in

economic-social ghettos—that is to say, that the costs of living in any particular suburban development can only be met by a certain income group (those of greater income presumably eschewing suburbs of lower income for reasons of prestige, and so on), thereby automatically excluding that mixture of economic (and hence, social) levels which provides a large part of the variety and life-quickening tensions of urban life. Furthermore, it is assumed that suburban developments are most often restricted by their developers or by their inhabitants against those of different race or color.

Levittown would seem to prove this assumption true. The deviation from an average income of $9,000 per year is almost nonexistent. Very few Levittowners earn less than that, fewer still earn more. About 60 per cent of Levittown's wage earners work in New York—overwhelmingly in white-collar jobs. (The fact that another 40 per cent work in Long Island within easy driving distance of home explodes a subsidiary myth about suburban employment's dependence on the big city—increasingly it depends not on the metropolis but on the megalopolitan matrix.) The ethnic composition of the community reflects the advances made in social intergroup relations as of about 1945. That is to say, religious bias is all but nonexistent; Protestants, Catholics and Jews mingle with the same social freedom they experienced in New York. But Levittown is very definitely a white ghetto. Negroes and Puerto Ricans are not welcome. When Negro veterans first attempted to buy houses in Levittown (in 1947 and 1949), they were turned away. They (and later influxes of Puerto Ricans) are still being turned away. For although discrimination in housing is now illegal, there are too many ways in which homeowners and realtors can discourage prospective purchasers for such anti-discrimination laws to be policed. Eventually, the largest roadblock against desegregation in such suburbs as Levittown is simply its reputation as being unreceptive to would-be Negro and Puerto Rican settlers.

Racial and economic conformity seem confirmed by the Levittown experience. What of aesthetic conformity, the accusation most often brought to bear against mass suburban developments? The Levitts, profiting from nineteenth century experience in designing "garden suburbs," owed much of their profits to their use of the suburban superblock as the basis of Levittown's layout. This area (much larger than a standard city block), today the basis of almost all suburban design, eliminates many costly construction factors, such as miles of additional streets and curbing and unnecessarily heavy paving on those streets which are provided. By making access to houses through narrower, less heavily paved (because they are less heavily used) cul-de-sac or U-turn streets and limiting through traffic to broader streets or highways around the superblock, not only is money saved, but space, too. This space can, in turn, be used for playgrounds, greens, more spacious residential plots.

But despite the advantages of the superblock, it is in itself no guarantee against a dreadful conformity in suburban landscapes. That would depend upon low density of habitation, variety of design and imaginative landscaping. These factors are in themselves expensive, however, and Levittown was built (as the large majority of suburban developments are built) to provide housing at low cost and still make a profit. The Levitts are to be congratulated on the fact that they did not lay out their development on the drearily familiar straight-line grid pattern of streets. Levittown's streets curve and turn, so that the vista down one of them is not a straight line into infinity but a closed view of houses and shrubbery. The Levitts also provided four different styles of houses among their prefabricated Cape Cods and ranch-styles. Furthermore, there is nothing in the Levittown zoning ordinances to prevent individual owners from altering their houses structurally and painting them whatever color they like, or developing their small gardens in any way that suits their fancy. In fact it would be very difficult to find fault (given the economic circumstances) with the provisions for and possibilities of nonconformity built into the Levittown development. And yet the overwhelming impression given by Levittown is one of extremely rigid architectural conformity.

Levittown's streets curve—but they curve in a repetitious pattern that makes one street indistinguishable from another. Levittown's houses have indeed been altered in very many cases by their owners—but they have almost all been altered in the same way (necessarily so, since additions are dictated by the basic design and structure of the house). Levittown dwellings are indeed painted in different colors—but the choice seems to have been most restricted, and in any event the sameness of architecture (the dominant picture window, the attached garage, the single staring eye of an "expansion attic" dormer) subdues what-

*Levittown,
suburban nursery*

ever variety might be provided by distinctive color.

Even more painfully conformist are Levittown's public buildings. They are all built in a style that can only be described as functionally deceptive modern with the single notable exception of the new public library, a bright and original structure. Levittown's schools (there are fifteen) look like Levittown's civic centers; Levittown's hospitals and clinics look like Levittown's schools and civic centers. They are uniformly built of red brick and glass without any attempt at either architectural originality or outside decoration. Furthermore, most of them are set in vast and barren fields of baked grass in summer and wind-driven snow in winter. The provision of open space for children and adults, so lacking in the city, has here been carried to an extreme which defeats its purpose. The solitary human being feels as unrelated and isolated in these vast and lonely meadows, unrelieved by any attempt at imaginative landscaping and dominated by structures which disguise their functions, as he might in one of New York's glass skyscraper canyons.

Levittown's commercial structures are zoned out of the residential districts, thereby robbing those districts of potential variety, and grouped in vast shopping centers. The design of these centers (the supermarket, the clothing store, the mail-order department store outlet, the liquor shop, the movie theater—all embracing a huge field of black tarmac) is as antihuman and abominable in Levittown as it is everywhere else in the United States. The one giant structure, providing (with the exception of ephemeral advertising displays) the same architectural outlet and expression for many varieties of products, goods and services, reduces even this lowest level of self-expression (buying and selling things) to an all but automated uniformity.

The historical suburb, it will be recalled, was an attempt to secure privacy for the expression of private life. This ideal was, however, swamped out of existence by its very attractiveness. Overcrowding in suburban development (of which symptom Levittown is by no means the worst example) leads to many of the same ills as city congestion: uniformity of design, shoddiness of construction, impoverishment of the public sector and a conformist, antlike way of life. Living in a large hive of an apartment house, knowing that every apartment above and below you is exactly like yours, is not very different from living in a suburb in which every house in sight is exactly like yours with a small space between.

But Levittown was not built precisely for the historical reasons that impelled nineteenth-century suburban development. People moving into it were seeking, first of all, housing—any kind of housing at rents they could afford. They were also fleeing city congestion, but they were not really seeking privacy in the sense that earlier suburbanites understood it. They were happy to settle for the fact that no neighbors lived above or below them; they could make almost all the noise they wanted. But their picture windows were surrounded by other picture windows; much less than a stone's throw away the neighbors inhabited identical structures. The density of development encouraged such impositions upon privacy as neighborly pressure to cut one's grass, paint one's house, *not* rent or sell to ethnic groups of which the majority disap-

proved and so forth. In fact, so great is the social pressure toward conformity in the new middle-income suburbs (and so obvious) that one must conclude that the twentieth-century suburbanite actually seeks them. Coming from the hive (any congested city), he does not feel wholly secure outside a hivelike environment.

It may be urged that residents of such suburban developments as Levittown cannot afford the larger land areas needed for privacy or for more personally designed homes, both because they lack the income and because they cannot afford increased isolation from their jobs. This is true. But what of their response to institutional and commercial conformity in architecture and design? Presumably, once a community is established, its public buildings ought to satisfy the tastes and requirements of the majority of its inhabitants, as should its commercial centers. In the case of public buildings (schools, civic centers, hospitals) the community may exert pressure politically, through approving or disapproving bond issues to finance any particular construction, through voting for or against municipal officials insofar as they support humane design and logical function in public architecture. In the case of commercial centers, public reaction can be much more swift and severe: simple avoidance. The surest way to discourage the dreadful shopping-center complexes that fester across the American countryside, but especially in the suburbs, would be to boycott their wares.

But here we come to a melancholy reexamination of the one assumption about suburbia that Levittown seemed to negate: lack of civic participation. On taking another look at the functions of Levittown's many civic organizations one soon discovers that they concern themselves with their environment only on the lowest level. A few years ago, one such organization devoted most of its energies for many months to successfully placing luminescent house numbers on the curbs for about two thousand homes. They did not devote their energies to fighting for imaginative school design or humane landscaping of public areas. There are more than a few Levittown organizations devoted to constant supervision of school curricula (PTA meetings are endless, school board elections bitterly fought); but no organization has ever been formed in Levittown to demand the kind of rezoning which would bring a few shops within walking distance, thereby introducing some color and variety into uniform neighborhoods and perhaps driving the grotesque shopping centers out of business. There was, a few years ago, a movement afoot to urge rezoning to allow industry to establish itself in Levittown. But this was motivated by such considerations as the desire to shift increasingly heavy tax loads onto industry. In any event this would have blotched, not improved, the environment.

But none of this proves that suburbanites like Levittowners do not desire a more varied, more colorful, more humane environment. For in a very real sense inhabitants of suburban developments are trapped in an environment which they have few means of changing. Levittown was privately developed, and its areas were planned in advance of construction. Zoning regulations had been wrested from Nassau County officials before the first bulldozer appeared. These zoning regulations were, of course, intended to set aside strictly residential neightborhoods. Once constructed and inhabited, any neighborhood resists change (if a shop is to be built, next to whose house will it be constructed?). Furthermore, the public buildings of such suburbs as Levittown are to a large extent beyond the control of its inhabitants. For example, so urgent was the problem of building and then increasing school space that any attempt to obstruct construction (however bleak) because of aesthetic considerations would have been overwhelmed by impatience. Likewise, unwilling to pay the taxes necessary to build and control a civic center, Levittowners received one as the gift of the Levitt family—and inhabitants were not disposed to look this gift-building in the mouth. Finally, to effect change, even today, Levittowners would have to wage a campaign directed not at their nonexistent immediate political identity, but at a very complex and remote series of entities, mostly county and state, which actually control their environment.

Thus, if Levittowners seem willing, perhaps even eager, to accept an antihuman uniformity in their environment (and we will examine later the suburban and nonsuburban impulses for and impact of this condition), it would be well to remember that in any event they are very largely *prisoners* of that environment with but little opportunity of changing it. They may be likened to the inhabitants of a large apartment house in any metropolis who, in an excess of civic zeal, might perhaps decide to make a contribution to their environment by painting, remodeling and decorating the exterior of their building: they would very quickly learn that they could not afford to do it themselves—and that there was no public channel whatsoever through which they could force their landlord to do it.

4 The Megalopolitan Matrix

*So great are the consequences of the general evolution
heralded by the present rise and complexity of
Megalopolis that an analysis of this region's problems
often gives one the feeling of looking at the dawn of a new
stage in human civilization.*

—JEAN GOTTMANN

The "dawn of a new stage" or the twilight of a civilization? Experts disagree violently as to which phenomenon megalopolis really represents. Some hold that this
vast "filling-in" of space with urban and suburban
forms, along with their transportation and commercial
tentacles, must lead to a wholly new concept of what
a city (and, by inference, what a noncity) is. To these
more optimistic urbanists, megalopolis describes a
new and presumably "higher" stage of reintegration
of human life, based on recent scientific conquests of
time, space and distribution. But many urban critics
hold that megalopolis is merely a word used to disguise both urban and rural disintegration into formlessness; and formlessness, these critics point out, is

defined in nature as death. But both sets of critics agree about one thing: namely, that suburbia's true general environment today is no longer "the fringe of the city" nor "the countryside near a city"—it is megalopolis. And just as the spread of suburbia helped give rise to megalopolis, so megalopolis increasingly produces new suburban phenomena. So new (and so startling) are some of these phenomena that to recognize them, one must retire the very word "suburban" to its original meaning. That is, in megalopolis "suburb" does not necessarily mean a defined area such as the older railroad suburb (Yonkers) or even the new suburban development (Levittown); it means any place of human habitation that is simply "less than urban." Which may simply be another way of saying that the suburban phenomena emerging within megalopolis can be defined as "human habitation without civic form."

What this formlessness means physically, in the eastern megalopolitan region, must be apparent to anyone who has attempted to find the limits of the New York Metropolitan Area (an area today not dissimilar on its fringes to the Los Angeles, Chicago, Boston or Houston metropolitan areas). Leaving the city toward the east (through Long Island) along the older routes (that is, not on parkways zoned to insulate drivers from their environment but on open roads) it is not possible to discover the city's limits. Like almost all other American cities of whatever size, New York to the east disintegrates into an endless no man's land of roadside "strip development." Here are the miles upon miles of secondhand auto lots; the neon-lighted roadside diners and hamburger stands;

the occasional empty lots used as trash heaps; the plywood shacks that house the people who work in the hamburger stands; the old farmhouses coated with aluminum and converted into restaurants or drive-ins or bars; the shopping centers catering to city, not suburb or country dwellers (you know you're out of the city when such centers display huge signs declaring "Buy here and escape the city sales tax!"). The development is continuous—it merges insensibly into country townships like Hempstead and Babylon all through Nassau County. These formerly defined towns become merely "wide spots" in strip development; and the strip development extends farther and farther beyond them. On U.S. Route 1 (the old Boston Post Road) strip development dribbles northeastward from the Bronx to merge into Greenwich, Connecticut, beyond Greenwich to merge into Stamford, beyond Stamford through Bridgeport, into New Haven—and ever north until the tentacles of the New York Metropolitan Area embrace those extending south from the Boston Metropolitan Area. There are, of course, islands of order and visual relief along the route, formed by the fringe residential areas of smaller towns and cities which have not been gobbled up entirely by roadside commerce. But essentially there is no "countryside," no break in intensive commercial cultivation of the environment between New York and Boston. A visitor from outer space might well imagine that both of these giant cities were simply twin "downtown" districts of one giant urban mass.

Upon what is this strip development based? How is it organized? To what does it owe its existence and its form (or lack of form)? To answer the easiest question first, it is unorganized in any meaningful civic sense. Only the fact that roadside commerce pays taxes to the townships through which it seeps, or, more often, to the county or state through which it crawls, places it within any civic jurisdiction at all. In fact, where strip development begins, just at the edge of cities large or small, a great part of the attraction to such commercial enterprise as used-car lots, junkyards, diners, and so on is the fact that urban zoning ordinances (and regulations) do not exist to curb exploitation of the environment (even in the limited sense that most city zoning ordinances may be said to curb it). Here the most atrocious degradation of the environment may take place happily free of building and land-use codes, except for those sparse and vague and rarely enforced statutes which the county or state may once have enacted. Those who conduct or are employed in roadside commerce often reside either in the city itself or in towns along the route, at a comfortable distance from their employment. Whatever civic allegiance they may have is dedicated to the areas in which they live, not the road along which they toil. That is simply a place from which a living must be wrested at no matter what cost to the environment. And for those forced to live within the area of strip development, there is no immediate authority below the county or state level to which they might apply (even if they wanted to) for relief from befoulment of their immediate surroundings.

As to why strip development has come into existence, to what it owes its spread; the answers are not so simple as they might appear. It is obvious to say that strip development is based on commercial catering to motorists. So heavy is the traffic between urban centers, large or small, within the megalopolitan region that profit may be extracted from that traffic's needs even though gasoline service stations sprout every half mile, roadside diners around every other bend, shopping clusters all but merge into one another along the route. In this sense strip development may be said to be one of the altars at which Americans worship the Automobile. But roadside commerce does not cater only to through roadside traffic. As suburban development seizes land areas more and more remote from city or town, the nearest highway becomes that suburb's shopping district. Thus, even though the overwhelming majority of through-traffic vehicles between Boston and New York no longer travel U.S. 1 but follow the much broader, better designed and speedier New England Throughway, there has been no diminution in the strip commercialization of the Boston Post Road; on the contrary, new roadside construction is much in evidence. But just as every city and town along the route is fringed by shopping centers more compact and easily reached than shopping clusters farther out along the highway, so almost every suburban development today comes complete with a shopping center to cater specifically to its needs. Why then would sufficient numbers of people bypass local shopping centers in sufficient numbers to support an ever expanding roadside commerce? A tentative guess (and it can be no better than a guess) might be the very nature of roadside commerce. Small, intensely competitive, various, vulgar in shabbiness or in newness, highly differentiated in architectural design and decoration, vivid in the conscious or unconscious humor of its advertising displays, it offers a welcome relief from and contrast to the massive impersonality of unified shopping centers. Driven from individualized shopping districts of cities and towns by the difficulty of finding parking space, many Americans apparently bypass institutionalized shopping centers to seek the same more personalized, more individual shopping experience of the now inaccessible "downtown" along the highway. Whether or not the subconscious search for variety and vitality in shopping may explain the continued expansion of highway strip development in megalopolis despite state and federal insulation of through traffic, the continuous road of small commerce is one of the most obvious physical aspects of the region.

Another inescapable physical aspect of the megalopolitan region is its massive manufacturing establishment—an establishment that forms more of the general environment of suburbia than is generally supposed. To the south of New York City, for example, stretching across the flatlands of New Jersey until it merges imperceptibly with Philadelphia's outer manufacturing ring is one of the nation's heaviest concentrations of industry (only that of the Chicago megalopolitan area is greater). This industrial center, along with that of New England, is the oldest in the nation. Both the proximity of the Pennsylvania coalfields and the density of population were factors in its growth, but the most important cause was undoubtedly the easy access to ocean transportation combined with excellent river and canal routes into the interior. Despite the fact that much manufacturing continues to leave the area for regions offering lower wage rates (the New England textile industry is a classic example) or lower taxes or simply more rational environments in an age of instantaneous communication and extra-rapid transportation, the physical manufacturing plant of megalopolis as a whole still dominates much of its landscape and is even growing (though at a much slower rate than such newer areas as the Southwest).

People living in northern New Jersey, if they commute to New York or to Philadelphia to work, may be said to be suburban to either of these huge cities. But the suburban areas they inhabit (be they engulfed small towns, older railroad suburbs, or suburban developments) do not exist in "countryside." Their immediate environment is much more likely to be the sprawl of industrial districts that dominates the New Jersey landscape (the same may be said of suburbanites living between New York and Boston). And since so much of the industry of this area is both heavy (primary metals, metal products, petroleum, chemical and rubber products) and old (many of the factories date from 1900) the suburban environment just beyond the screen of trees or the linked fence or across the highway is a nineteenth-century Industrial Revolution nightmare.

What this can mean becomes glaringly clear if one attempts to find anything remotely identifiable as a classically evolved suburb as one leaves New York to the south, over the Hudson. The river's existence imposes an automatic boundary on New York City's expansion in that direction; there is no sense of the city straggling out into other areas. Instead there are the older jurisdictional urban centers of Jersey City, Newark and Trenton, each large enough to support

its own suburban development as well as to dominate the New York–Philadelphia suburban environment. These places are referred to as "jurisdictional urban centers" rather than "cities" because by no rational definition of what a city is supposed to be may they be described as such. They are hubs for massive concentrations of industry, barracks quarters for the workers in those industries, out-of-date industrial coketowns. For miles in any direction around them extend blackened, soot-begrimed factory districts; a tangle of (mostly) decaying factory buildings, old railroad spurs, warehouses, chemical and petroleum storage tanks, electric power stations and cables, tall chimneys spewing filth into the air and small streams choked with industrial waste. Just as Jersey City, Newark and Trenton merge their factory surroundings, so they merge their smog. In fact, New York City's smog merges with the industrial fumes of northern New Jersey which in turn merge eventually with the acrid clouds enveloping Philadelphia to form a regional and inescapable mid-Atlantic smog belt.

It is within this noisome, foul-smelling, eye-searing landscape that much suburban development has taken place over the last seventy years. Older, more gracious New Jersey towns along the Atlantic Coast, the pleasant countryside of Bucks County, Pennsylvania (at about the extreme commuting-distance limit from New York), were long ago converted into railroad suburbs. Because of the older zoning laws in many of these communities, or simply because of natural chance, such as the interposition of hills or nondeveloped "wasteland," residents may be somewhat insulated from their general coketown environment, though commuters must inescapably pass through it. But no such insulation is granted (or, apparently, sought) by the numberless small suburban land developments that fester along the highways between New York and Philadelphia. Here, possibly because of lower land values and cheaper tax rates, are to be found (much more so than on Long Island or to the north of New York City) the drab "model-prison"-type suburban exploitations. Here are the suburbs with rigid checkerboard street plans, shabby plywood houses each exactly like the next, no land whatsoever set aside for community or public purposes, no attempt made to inform life with civic interest or participation. Many of these military-camp suburban developments do not even boast a shopping center; such centers are built equidistant from several of them to service all. And, of course, commercial highway strip development engulfs the routes along which they are built. In terms of where the majority of their residents earn their living, these developments may be said to be suburban to New York or Trenton or Jersey City or Philadelphia—or, more likely, they may be suburban to the proximate industrial wasteland. But actually they are not suburban to any city in the sense of being a far-flung residential expression of an urban pattern. Instead they are simply noncivic housing developments sprouting weedlike in vacant little enclaves amid industrial districts.

The factory wasteland of megalopolis is, however, changing both in content and form. The older heavy industries have been giving way, statistically, to light industries, service industries, research facilities and distribution centers. Factories themselves are often designed today with some care for their outer appearances. They are often set in large, open parklike areas. Some slight effort is even made to harmonize their structure with the surrounding architecture or natural landscape. But until rational definitions of land use (the reasonable demarcation of townships, city boundaries, suburban developments, open public parkland and industrial districts) can be imposed on the vast confusion of megalopolitan development, even the newer industrialization brings, and will continue to bring, blight to large areas.

A case in point is to be found north of New York City, following the Hudson River beyond Yonkers through the small towns (older railroad suburbs after the turn of the century) to the limits of easy commutation to New York. These limits may be located in the group of villages known as the Tarrytowns, clustered at the river around the eastern terminal of the New York State Throughway's Tappan Zee Bridge, which spans the Hudson about fifty-five miles north of New York City. Fifty-five miles may not seem to be a commutation limit in terms of distance; but in terms of time, either on the New York Central Railroad or in fighting through traffic funneled into the city by parkway and throughway, it is certainly a limit.

The Tarrytowns (Tarrytown, North Tarrytown and Irvington) are steeped in history and tradition. This is the region of Washington Irving's "Sleepy Hollow," of the old Dutch manor houses and farms, of the Revolutionary War escapades of Major André and Benedict Arnold. Like Yonkers, it was part of the Philipse estate before the Revolution and much attention and effort has been expended (with the help of the Rockefeller Foundation) to restore and preserve the historical sites and landmarks of the area. Until the 1850s, the Tarrytowns remained sleepy Hudson River ports for the shipment of farm produce downriver to New York City. Manufacturing was limited to boots and shoes and pottery. But with the arrival of the New York Central Railroad (then known as the Hudson River Railroad) in 1849, the Tarrytowns became railroad suburbs of New York. Because the time required to reach the city was too great for employees who had to report to work on time in the days when factory and office hours commenced at 7:30 A.M. and ended at 7:30 P.M., the Tarrytowns became a railroad suburb of the very rich, who often did not have to report to work at all. Huge and beautiful homes were built by the Tiffanys, the Morgans, the Cottinets, the Harpers and the Fargos—all families prominent in American industry, commerce and finance.

As American prosperity diffused to broader segments of the population, more people could afford to live in Tarrytown; but the number was never very great. By 1950 the total population of Tarrytown, North Tarrytown and Irvington still did not exceed 21,000 people— a few of them local artisans or caterers to the suburban residents, but the great majority of them true suburbanites of greater means than their brethren in Yonkers or Levittown. And it would seem that in this suburban case, money had bought the best that suburbia could offer: a beautiful natural environment in the rolling countryside along the Hudson, seclusion from congestion (few could afford to live there), distance not only from the disorderly metropolis but also from the industrial complex spotted throughout the region. True, the natural waterfront of the Tarrytowns

was cut off and mangled by the New York Central Railroad tracks—but there were areas beyond the tracks where one could stroll or fish or keep small boats. The ferry to Nyack across the river was pleasant in itself and enhanced rather than blighted the charm of the environment. The "downtown" districts of the villages were (and remain) in a sad state of decay— but so small were the communities that downtown blight did not seriously affect residents or the overall attractiveness of the towns.

Then, during the early 1950s, the omnipotent New York State Highway Commission, in association with the federal government, decreed that the New York State Throughway would pass through Tarrytown— furthermore, that its only bridge across the Hudson would be built just there. This was not a shattering assault on Tarrytown's isolation—the Saw Mill River Parkway had for years provided mass automobile access to the region. Nor did the throughway engineers plan (as they did in so many cases) to destroy the communities by bulldozing their huge concrete highway through the center of either commercial or residential districts—the throughway would skirt the Tarrytowns' southern edge and then leap the river. Nor can it be said that the Tappan Zee Bridge, when opened in 1956, proved to be in itself an ugly, dominating structure. On the contrary, it was graceful and as unobtrusive as possible. Yet the routing of the throughway next to Tarrytown and the opening of the bridge brought disaster to the area as a residential suburban region.

The throughway attracted new industry to the area, which now combined rapid truck and motor transport facilities with cheap river transport. The new industries were not ancient nineteenth-century-type factories. They were rationally designed, modern plants—specifically, the car assembly plants of Chevrolet and Fisher Body Divisions of General Motors Corporation. By the nature of their work, these plants do not pump vast amounts of smog into the atmosphere, nor do they pollute the Hudson River to any great extent. The buildings are low, not domineering; there is not a smokestack in sight and only one water tower. These plants (and several smaller groups) are examples of *new* megalopolitan industrialization, constructed with a conscience about potential industrial corruption of the environment.

Yet their existence (along with that of the throughway) has effectively destroyed the residential-suburban character of the communities. First of all, the population of the Tarrytowns rose from 8,000 to 16,000 in less than six years, the increase being accounted for by workers in the new plants. And this called for new housing—provided both by small suburban "development" areas and by the intrusion of apartment houses not far from the plants. But this increase in residential population is misleading; to it must be added an increase in the nonresidential population during working hours. The new plants drew workers and office personnel from nearby towns and also (its top management) from New York City (thus, by one definition of the term, making New Yorkers suburbanites of Tarrytown!). This in turn imposed heavier loads on Tarrytown's traffic facilities. But with admirable foresight, the new plants had provided for that by opening spur roads connecting to the throughway and the parkway

and by providing vast parking lots next to the plants
themselves.

The total result has been that the very consumption
of land (all of it precious waterfront property) for
industry, traffic and parking has effectively turned the
Tarrytown riverfront into an industrial park. The
older New York Central riverfront mangling could be
overlooked to a certain extent because it was, after

all, a narrow strip easily crossed. But the new plants consume too much space and their construction extends for acres all along and right down to the water's edge.

This modern industrialization, carried out with care and foresight, has ruined the preceding environment. It may be, of course, that in an over-all, regional view, the Tarrytown area should be converted into one large industrial park with only "efficient" housing units for those workers who must live near the plants. But this is certainly not the end desired by the residents of the Tarrytowns, and this is not the end forecast by any regional plan. For the fact is that there is no regional plan for this area or for any other area within megalopolis. And until such a plan comes into being, with proper zoning for industry, suburbs, towns, smaller cities and the great metropolises as well as parklands and transportation routes, then no matter how careful the planning or how thoughtful the design, the suburbanization of manufacturing and the movement of industry within the entire region will continue to bring haphazard blight to new environments. All this will be considered later. Meanwhile, taking a broad view of the megalopolitan matrix in which suburbia nestles, with its tentacles of commercial strip development, its merging of towns and cities, its industrial wastelands, its helter-skelter of suburban and sub-suburban developments, its general formlessness and lack of differentiation, it is hard not to agree with those critics who, like Lewis Mumford, hold that megalopolis is neither a new, higher stage of urban civilization, nor the prelude to such a stage, but is itself the symptom of a mortal disease in our civilization.

5 The Internal Combustion Conspiracy

Commuter—one who spends his life
In riding to and from his wife;
A man who shaves and takes a train
And then rides back to shave again.
                    —E. B. WHITE

Mr. White was, of course, referring to a fast-vanishing species: the suburbanite willing or able to travel by train. This subgroup of *homo sapiens* is almost as extinct now as is that other subphylum, the pedestrian. The destruction of commuter passenger service on American railways has been a mutual operation of commuters and railroad officials, egged on by highway engineers and automobile manufacturers, all of whom seem so dedicated to one single mode of transportation —that provided by the internal combustion engine— as to suggest a conspiracy. It is not, of course, a conspiracy—it is simply stupidity in the service of the gods of Power, Expansion and Greed.

Not that there is necessarily any evil inherent in the

motorcar or truck. They may be dangerous, obsolete in conception and inefficient for many purposes; but there are certain functions performed by both private and commercial motor transport which are desirable, perhaps even essential. The evil lies not in the machine, nor even necessarily in that essential concomitant machine, the paved road or highway; it lies in the simpleminded worship of these instruments which, more than any other single mechanical factor, has produced the formless chaos of megalopolis and transformed the suburb, once a refuge from congestion and uniformity, into an even bleaker environment than the central city.

Not that the machines themselves do not merit some criticism. American cars are notoriously too large, overpowered, underengineered. True efficiency in automotive manufacture has been sacrificed to the shibboleths of speed, pretentiousness and envy. More importantly, true efficiency in the entire concept of motor transport would have long since provided *differentiated* means to achieve different ends. A large high-speed vehicle may be ideally suited to roaring down a throughway at seventy miles per hour to transport a family from one city to another or from their home to some distant objective; such a vehicle is utterly unsuited to use *within* cities. The recent heavy importation of small, easily maneuverable and parkable European cars indicates that city dwellers, at least, are beginning to exchange pretentiousness for efficiency. But these remain only a small proportion. Meanwhile the suburbanite is faced with a hard choice: either he buys a large American car with which to rush down the highways from suburb to city and then spends hours trying to maneuver through congested streets and find parking space for his behemoth, or he buys a small car suited to the city but not really well suited to the expressway he must traverse to get there. But the very fact that he is presented with this choice indicates a much more important degree of insanity within the overall concept of modern transportation.

Transportation, to be rational, ought to be a function of human needs. And human needs, by their very nature, are different. To provide only one mode of transport to fulfill these needs is monomaniacal. For example, to transport large numbers of suburbanites over distances of about seventy miles to the heart of the city, no better means has ever been devised than the railroad. It occupies but little land, is capable of reasonable speed, does not congest the countryside or the city and, above all, delivers people to the rapid-transit facilities of the city itself. It is objected that suburban rail lines are notoriously delapidated, slow and not sufficiently diffused to serve a wide area. But all these criticisms only imply that available (long since available) technology has not been applied to rail transportation. Trains can now be built to travel more than two hundred miles per hour; they can be suspended from cables (thereby eliminating the costly roadbed track-laying process); they have long since been electrified in many areas (thereby eliminating smog production) and can be made as comfortable and silent as anyone wants. But America's entire railroad system (not just the suburban routes) has been allowed to decay to the near-vanishing point. To resuscitate it now, rationalize it, will require an exceptionally large public investment; private railroad ownership has long since demonstrated its incapacity to deal with the problems.

Another example is the death of inland waterway passenger transportation. In many areas of the country this is a highly feasible way to travel. In the megalopolitan East, with its many navigable rivers and canals, water transport could prove more efficient than either auto or rail. For example, the suburban inhabitants of much of Long Island and of the entire Hudson River Valley might well travel to and from New York City by water routes. They used to, not many decades ago. But the old Hudson River side-wheelers proved too slow, small and cumbersome to appease the insatiable demand for speed and more speed. For years now, however, new technology has offered new solutions to river and canal transport—most notably high-speed hydrofoil boats. A few of these are already in use (especially in Seattle) or about to enter experimental use. They can be constructed to almost any size (huge, oceangoing hydrofoils are now planned for trans-Atlantic traffic and freight), can go at remarkable speeds, can carry numerous passengers in comfort and, like trains, can deliver them to city rapid-transit systems. In addition they have access to all the older suburban towns and cities which were originally built along water transport routes.

These examples are, of course, based on the terrible impact of the suburban motorcar upon the cities; they offer some possible means of halting the daily motor invasion of urban centers. But what about the tyranny of mono-transportation in the suburbs themselves? Older railroad suburbs or suburbs which are centered upon small towns have, like large cities, permitted their public transit facilities to deteriorate to the vanishing point. The new suburban developments are rarely provided with any means of public transit whatsoever. Yet in the case of the older suburbs, residential districts have developed in rings farther and farther from the central town's shopping, community and service facilities. In the case of the newer suburban developments, zoning regulations have forbidden the introduction of these facilities into residential districts. The only public means of transport provided with any efficiency to carry passengers to necessary ends is generally the schoolbus system. Suburbanites are thus made absolutely dependent upon their cars to perform necessary errands such as shopping or reaching railroad or intercity bus stations, or getting to a hospital or a movie theater.

The solution offered by suburban developers to this problem has been the shopping center. This means (in the average suburb) that to buy groceries or a package of cigarettes, suburbanites are expected to drive two or three miles and then (on a busy day) park their cars on an asphalt plain (sweltering in summer, icy in winter), to walk the rest of the way to their destination over a longer distance than the average city dweller must traverse to walk all the way to his nearest store! Where the objective is not a shopping center, but rather the downtown district of a town-centered suburb, the suburbanite runs into parking difficulties (and traffic congestion) almost as severe as those encountered by city dwellers.

All of which may be said to be the fault of zoning and design, not of the transport system. But suburban zoning and planning have been engineered precisely

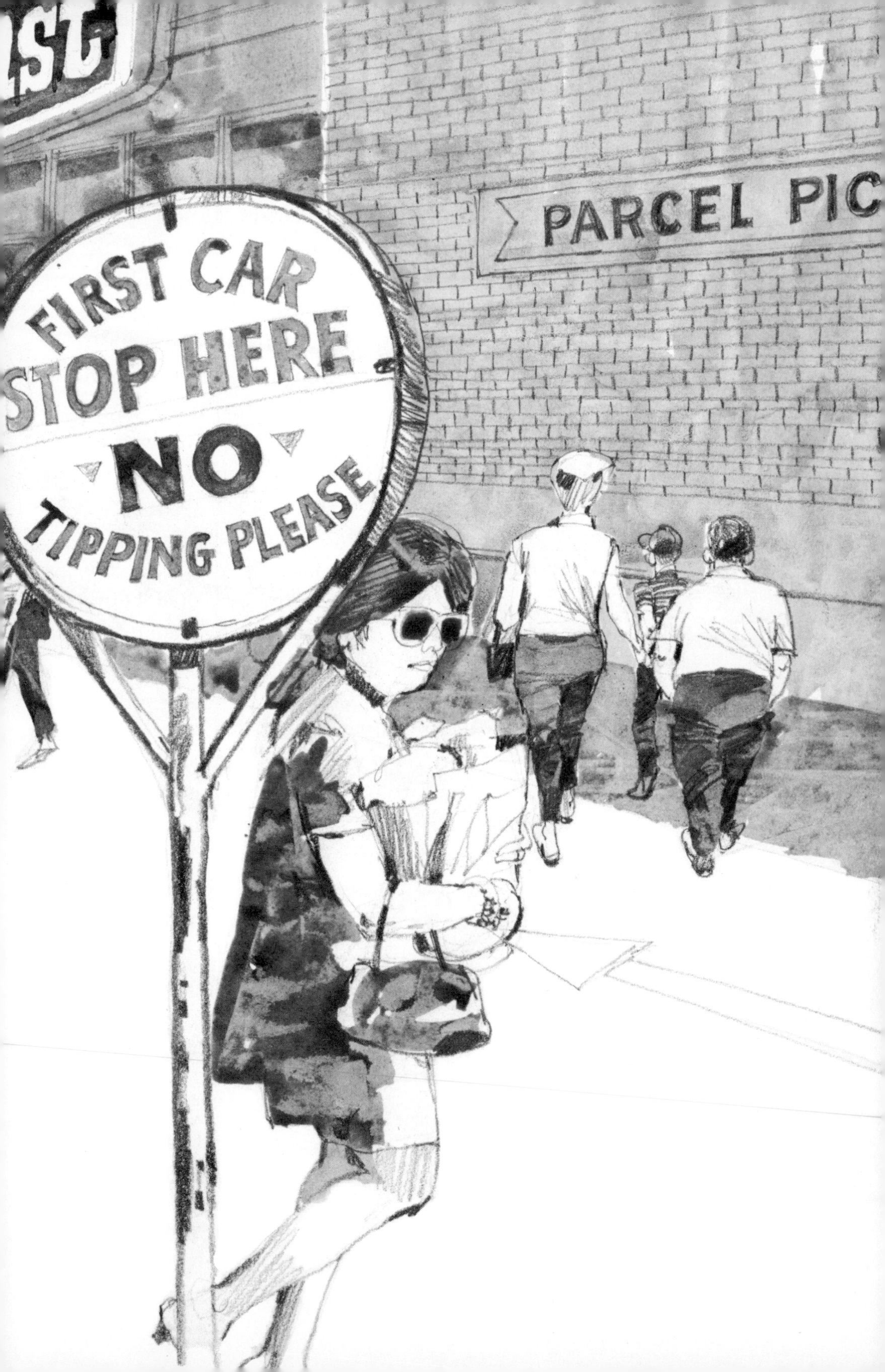
FIRST CAR
STOP HERE
NO
TIPPING PLEASE
PARCEL PIC

on the basis of (and to take advantage of) private auto transportation. This in itself has led to a far more serious blight than shopping centers. It has led to giantism in the suburbs. Before the advent of the motorcar, not only were the older railroad suburbs limited in number (to the railroad stops), they were also limited in size, more or less within the pedestrian scale. Few of the New York suburbs before 1910 numbered more than 9,000 inhabitants—this representing in population the land area compassable by walking for various errands or to visit neighbors. But the motorcar not only spread suburbs all over the countryside; it made feasible a huge increase in the size of those suburbs. And with this increase in size, accompanied by low-density building of individual homes on individual plots, the entire concept of a suburb as a self-contained residential community died. As suburbs expanded they merged into one another and such phenomena as the sub-suburban housing development began to appear. Form—the distinction between countryside, village, suburb and city—was sacrificed by and for motor transportation; and the vast formlessness of megalopolis has emerged.

Thus far we have discussed, really, only one-half of the internal combustion machine: the vehicle propelled by the engine itself. But there is another half —the road. Until (in the United States) well into the twentieth century, most roads and highways corresponded fairly closely to the old Roman road width of about sixteen feet. The advent of the motorcar and truck has, of course, changed all that. First, the old stagecoach routes like U.S. 1 and U.S. 66 (the Lincoln Highway) were paved, straightened and widened (to two autowide lanes). Until World War II, very few highways in America boasted more than a single lane in each direction. The exception to this statement was New York State and some of the immediate environment of New York City. The older, narrow highways had not been zoned for anything in particular. When cars began to increase on them to profitable numbers, they soon flourished with billboard and other advertisements, and strip development began. So hideous were the results (and so dangerous to motorists) that during the 1930s, in New York State, the concept of the parkway was born. This was to be a four-lane highway (two lanes in each direction) with a divider in the middle (grass and trees where possible, concrete where necessary) and acres of parkland on either side of the road from which both advertising and strip development were banished. Some of the parkways built in the East just before World War II, notably the Taconic State Parkway and the Saw Mill River Parkway, were superb examples of highway engineering, affording safe, well constructed and carefully planned roadbeds for cars; and providing delightful landscaped scenery both for the cars' occupants and for pedestrians. Furthermore, the parkland strip insulated the highway and its traffic from local communities around which the road passed.

But the road-as-machine is complementary to the motorcar, and the parkways of New York State and Connecticut were not built either to handle the stupendous increase in traffic which developed after World War II or the larger, more highly powered vehicles that poured from Detroit. Safe parkway speed is about fifty miles per hour at most; but sup-

plied with huge and powerful new toys, the American people demanded a chance to use them at the much higher speeds of which they were capable. The result was, at first, a development of wider roads with far fewer curves, generally called expressways. A few such were opened on Long Island, but Los Angeles is the natural breeding ground of this type of highway. Because of their width (ever increasing over the years from four to six to eight to twelve lanes, with the lanes themselves increasingly wider) and the amount of traffic they are meant to carry at the speeds it is hoped that traffic will achieve, there is no room to zone parkland on either side. Furthermore, in the interests of highway safety (again, at higher speeds and increased volume) expressways have been cut in bulldozed straight lines right through the vital tissues of our cities and through the not less vital tissues of suburban and open land beyond.

The idea of an expressway (one might call it a broad highway within the city and its immediate environs) —to carry the most cars at the highest speed from one urban or megalopolitan area to another, or to link up the state parkways—did not, however, provide any solution to interstate or long-distance travel. While broad parkways and expressways flourished or festered around cities like New York (the West Side Drive, the Cross-Bronx, the Cross-County, the Long Island), Chicago (the entire outer, outer-outer and outer-outer-outer drive complex beyond Lake Shore Drive) and Los Angeles (the conversion of former broad boulevards like Wilshire and La Brea), interstate traffic, which really had some rational need for speed over very long distances, struggled along on two, sometimes three-lane highways. Only in a few areas did large through-roads exist like the old Pensylvania Turnpike (in itself a combination parkway-expressway). All of this was changed, however, beginning in 1957, when the federal government, sharing costs with the states, decided to undertake the construction of a "National Defense Throughway" system of interstate roads, the most massive roadbuilding program in human history. Largely completed now, the continental throughway system, combined with the older parkways and expressways and surviving highways (many of the oldest routes were devoured by the new), provide our present motor transportation environment. What has that environment contributed specifically to suburbia and its megalopolitan matrix?

The first, most obvious answer is that it has opened larger and larger areas of countryside to more and more people. At throughway speeds (legally 65 miles per hour in the East but actually closer to 75 miles per hour) ever more distant regions and towns can be comfortably drawn within commutation range of the large cities or megalopolitan industrial complexes. In the older suburbs this has resulted in increased population densities which have all but wiped out former suburban advantages of open space and country environment. More than that, by opening everwidening reaches of countryside, it has encouraged land speculation and real-estate development of the lower class of suburban housing—filling in the open spaces between older suburbs with sub-suburbs ad infinitum.

Secondly, these huge roads take up an amazingly

large space of countryside themselves. It is generally realized that "space-eating" throughways have destroyed much of America's urban tissue (in Los Angeles, fully one-third of the city is devoted to throughway development, two-thirds of the former downtown district). But it is not as fully appreciated that the size of these highways has also devoured much rural tissue. The throughway or expressway itself spreads concrete over thousands and thousands of acres; but more thousands are devoured by the necessary concomitants of these roads—cloverleafs and interchanges. Beyond that, it is not simply the area covered in concrete which is blighted. The very existence of the throughway or expressway, with its roaring, smelly, dangerous traffic, makes land on both sides of the roadbed unfit for human habitation or recreation for miles in both directions.

This in itself might not be especially disturbing; after all, there are many areas of the country which are wasteland and through which such roads might be pushed with little damage to either human or natural environment. But almost inevitably the throughways and expressways have been bulldozed through precisely those areas where they can achieve the most baneful impact. Not satisfied with providing through routes between the largest cities of the nation, throughway and expressway engineers have attempted to link up smaller cities and towns into the national superhighway grid. To justify themselves, throughways must carry a tremendous load of traffic. But this tremendous load can only be achieved in densely settled areas. So the throughways have been pushed along the most heavily traveled routes, along the historic main roads between cities where their presence brings blight to vast suburban and small town populations. In many cases, not simply blight but total destruction is the result as the super-roads have been cut right through the middle of former communities. The supreme irony of throughway development has been that in very many cases, the throughways parallel the older railroad routes—inefficiently duplicating a decaying system and consuming, in the process, much more land than the railroads ever required.

A third result of the proliferation of superhighways throughout the megalopolitan region has been the encouragement of the dispersion of industry. With wide swaths of concrete spreading weblike through the countryside, more and more formerly inaccessible sites have become available to industrial development, sites to and from which both workers and freight can be moved by motor transport. At an earlier stage of megalopolitan development, this dispersion of industry seemed healthy. No longer chained to water routes or rail lines, factories could relocate farther from the older cities and towns, thereby removing one prime cause of urban blight. Not only did industrial dispersal promise a better urban environment, it also suggested an economic base upon which entire new communities or cities could be built, thereby alleviating urban congestion in the older centers.

Unfortunately, the promise of dispersion has not produced the desired results. A certain amount of urban congestion and blight has been relieved (at the price of decreasing the urban tax base and urban employment opportunities) and many of the dispersed industries or factories have provided themselves with

a much more humane environment (many are set in landscaped grounds, and, because of lower rural land values, have been able to achieve a more spacious and humane architecture). But however rational the design, the establishment of a huge factory does not enhance the immediate environment. Where such factories have been built in or very close to former rural towns (as in Tarrytown) they have destroyed suburban values; where they have been built on ex-wasteland, they have assured that their immediate surroundings will remain wasteland, unavailable for public parks or recreational areas. Furthermore, they have not provided the basis for new communities. Instead, in almost every case, they have provided an opportunity for the worst kind of speculative housing developments, suburban not to any organized civic entity but to the twin poles of factory and shopping center. The dispersion of industry made possible by the superhighway system has resulted only in increasing the formlessness of the entire megalopolitan region, speeding its transformation into one huge, undifferentiated mass of industry and housing in which the advantages of countryside, suburb, town and city are equally submerged.

It is sometimes urged that the development of a superhighway system in the United States has, at least, increased the personal freedom of Americans. As a people, Americans have always been "on the go," and the provision of cheap cars (relative to foreign standards) and huge highways have increased opportunities for personal movement. But actually the overemphasis on motor transport and the resultant decay of all other modes of transportation has increased

American freedom to travel by one means only; it has actually reduced the very important element of choice in means of movement, and is, furthermore, an extremely inefficient means of moving large masses of people. The average expressway or throughway can deliver but five or six thousand vehicles per hour (an average of ten or twelve thousand individuals) to any given point; the railroads, even in their present decayed condition without any of the newer technological advances possible, can deliver forty to sixty thousand people per hour. And although throughway traffic may move at speeds of over 65 miles per hour along the open road, congestion at terminal points is such that the average speed of movement from place to place is reduced to something closer to 30 miles per hour. Railroads *before the First World War* could *average* (even allowing for their many station stops) at least 50 miles per hour.

None of which even takes account of the terrible impact on both city and suburb of the delivery of thousands upon thousands of huge vehicles into their precincts. But this impact is only part of the overall symbiotic relationship between suburb, city and megalopolis to which we must now turn.

6 Impact and Rebound

*The dividing lines between town and country are even
now gradually disappearing as conditions are reversing
themselves. The country absorbs the life of the city
as the city shrinks to the utilitarian purpose that
now alone justifies its existence.*

FRANK LLOYD WRIGHT

Which is another way of saying that differentiation
and form disappear as megalopolis swallows both city
and suburb. But the process is complex, one of action
and reaction. For example, the simple assumption that
the city has been losing inhabitants to suburbia or ex-
urbia is not true. At one time (from about 1935 to
1955, especially in the immediate post-World War II
years) New York's population remained static, even
dipped slightly, which, given the natural birth rate
within the city, meant that many New Yorkers were
leaving. But recently this phenomenon has ceased,
New York's population has begun to grow again despite exodus to suburbia, and the *rate* of increase is
not solely attributable to the influx of Puerto Rican

migrants. The truth is that people are people, not statistics, and do not necessarily behave in predictable ways. Demographers and sociologists witnessing the flight to the suburbs of the 1940s and 1950s assumed that those who fled had fled for good. Yet such intangible, unmeasurable influences as simple boredom have caused an unexpected remigration to the city of many of those refugees. An inspection, therefore, of the mutual impacts of city and suburb and megalopolitan environment upon each other is a kaleidoscope of people and events in *motion;* today's image may be reversed tomorrow.

The first and most important relationship between city and suburb has been just this question of population shift. But to understand some of its paradoxes, we must understand some of its causes. American cities, unlike European, do not have their roots in a mythical, religious, aristocratic or even humanistic past. They were established and grew entirely on the basis of their efficiency as centers of trade, industry and commerce—their efficiency, that is, as machines with which individuals or groups might exploit their environment for personal or social gain. Thus the first population movement within what is now called megalopolis was from the countryside to the city, as the lure of the efficiency of the machine grew. During the nineteenth century not only did increasing numbers of rural folk move to urban centers, but immigrants from abroad stayed in urban centers rather than moving out into the countryside. From about 1867 to 1920 the means of exploitation offered by the city-as-machine was the burgeoning industrialization of the country. Industry grew in many cities (such as Pittsburgh, Chicago, Detroit) because of their geographic situation as regards raw materials and cheap water or railroad transportation. Processing industries, distribution industries and the great industry of managing and manipulating industries (banking and finance) grew in such centers as New York and Boston and Philadelphia not only because of their geographic situation as great Atlantic ports or centers from which inland waterways led to the interior, but also because of their previous success in concentrating successful preindustrial commerce.

All of which converted many American urban centers into factory districts—industrial coketowns filled with hideous manufacturing structures, noise, smog, pollution, barracks housing for workers, and so on. And those cities such as New York or Boston which escaped some of the heaviest industry and whose ultimate wealth rested not so much upon manufacture as upon management (although both these examples boasted industry enough to befoul air, water and environment) turned into gigantic office building centers where less and less provision was allowed for human habitation. As machines they might be less noisome than Pittsburgh or Detroit, but just as antihuman.

One of the basic foundations of the American economic and social structure has always been the assumption that the American environment existed for exploitation by the American people for their private gain. Large-scale investment in the public sector of the economy (one thinks of the port, road and canal building fever of the 1820s, of the railroad building era of the 1860s and 1870s; of the massive New Deal reconstruction of the 1930s) has almost always been devoted to increasing facilities and opportunities for private exploitation. Even the public school system grew not so much from any abstract love of learning or culture as from the necessity of equipping larger and larger sections of the population with the means of manipulating their environment—again on the assumption of private, not public, gain. One of the results of this outlook, which became most apparent after World War II, was that while cities had become extremely efficient exploitation machines, making more and more of their inhabitants wealthier and wealthier, they had become less and less fit places for human habitation. Devotion to the private sector of society had produced more, larger and flashier automobiles, all but fully automatic kitchens; the home entertainment center of television, and so forth. Miserliness toward the public sector had provided badly paved, refuse-littered, congested streets; disgracefully foul slums; overcrowded, understaffed and ill-equipped schools. So just as private means increased to the point where larger sections of the urban population could afford to escape, public squalor provided the impetus for them to do so.

It was this conjunction that produced the mass exodus from American cities during the 1940s and 1950s. But unfortunately the growth of private wealth had never included *all* the American people—even today, when the nation has reached a dizzy pinnacle of prosperity, fully one-third of its citizens live on the edge of poverty; before the Second World War close to half did so. But the poor, like other Americans, dreamed of partaking of the feast. Those who inhabited the cities remained there to try to win a niche in the exploitation machine; hundreds of thousands, ascending into millions, who were rural poor, moved to the cities with the same hopes. There, the overwhelming majority of them were and remain trapped —more aware now that they are among the raw materials fed into the urban exploitation machine, not its potential manipulators. So the exodus from urban centers was selective even though massive. Those who could afford to escape and had the impulse to do so were of the middle class; the rich had either long since escaped or were able through their wealth to insulate themselves within the cities against the worst aspects of their environment. The poor stayed behind in the increasingly squalid slums.

This had several effects upon American cities. First of all, it removed from their control an important amount of wealth—measured not only in the higher taxes middle-class people could pay, but also in their consumption of private and public services upon which much of the city's wealth depended. At the same time, the physical decay of much of the urban structure demanded higher taxes (and a wider tax base) for reconstruction. Along with this, both in absolute and relative terms, the amount of the city's wealth devoted to aiding the increasing percentage of poverty-stricken citizens rose alarmingly. Thus, from the urban viewpoint, the flight to the suburbs, which might have been a blessing in decongesting the cities, actually proved to be a disaster—the first and one of the most importantly disastrous impacts of suburbia upon American cities.

But this exodus had other impacts as well. First of all, those who left the city largely continued to work there. New York's nighttime population is about 7,800,000—but its daytime population ascends to 12,000,000 or more! This commuting population puts a massive strain upon city services such as police, sanitation, and rapid transit, but pays no municipal taxes to support them. Likewise, with the decay (as we have seen) of public transportation systems and the elevation of the motorcar into its present place of deified supremacy, cities have had to cut into their vital urban tissue to provide those space-eating expressways necessary to the daily influx of hundreds of thousands (in New York, millions) of private cars. City streets are converted into parking lots (increasingly, entire city areas are converted into parking lots) and so badly congested that the very efficiency of the city as an exploitation machine is lessened. Regional authorities (in the case of New York, the New York State Highway Commission and the semi-public Triborough Bridge and Port authorities) devote their energies to providing ever larger, ever faster means of access for commuters to urban centers without regard for municipal needs. City planners desperately attempting to bring some order into America's urban chaos are helpless before this suburban vehicle onslaught. So grotesque is the problem that hysterical solutions are sometimes offered—such as New York Mayor Lindsay's proposal to send the New York City Police simply to close the bridge and tunnel entrances into Manhattan!

Another, less direct impact of suburbia upon the city has been the flight from it of industry and commerce—both, again, essential to municipal taxes and municipal employment. While it is true that a booming national economy has increased in *absolute* terms the number of industries in New York City (they are no longer manufacturing plant gains, but commercial and management industry gains), the *relative* increase has fallen far behind that of the surrounding megalopolitan region. Furthermore, this increase has been in precisely those fields (advertising, communications, corporate management, finance) which offer few employment opportunities to the ill-educated, suppressed urban poor. The decay of older urban industrial districts, combined with increased traffic congestion, soaring tax rates and increasing complexity and sophistication in industrial processes, has caused a large scale exodus of industry from the city to suburban regions—and this not only for the advantages discussed previously, but also to take advantage of the fact that more and more people with the skills necessary to cope with ever more complicated industrial tasks reside no longer in the city but in its suburbs. So general has this exodus become that today it is no longer a question of manufacturing plants (whether heavy or light) or even of distributive establishments; now even the management facilities are moving away from the city as corporations increasingly seek a more rational environment both for their operations and their staff. Indeed, with the burgeoning of communications resources, there is little rationality behind any corporation's decision to locate its headquarters in any urban center—except, perhaps, for prestige, a notoriously fickle factor.

If these are some of the most glaringly disastrous

effects of suburbia's impact upon the city, what of the impact of the city on suburbia—and on the megalopolitan region? First of all, again, is the question of population shift. The city has poured millions of people into older suburbs and into the fast-vanishing countryside where new suburbs or sub-suburbs have been established. It must be remembered that these were not people seeking a completely rural life. They were not potential farmers, woodsmen or pioneers (all of which were, in any case, all but vanished occupations); they were people chained to the city by employment and economic necessity. Furthermore, though this has been little appreciated, they were people chained to the city by their entire background, lifestyles and ways of thinking. They were prosperous enough (relative to the urban poor) and frightened enough (by the antihuman urban environment) to flee the city's immediate precincts. They were not rich enough nor adventurous enough to leave it completely behind. Furthermore, and this is an important factor, they were not dedicated enough to civic ideals (which American life does little to foster) to remain in the cities and fight for their transformation into decent, humane environments. They were people forced and willing to settle for a modest improvement in their personal environment as a means of escaping from apparently hopeless decay of the public, civic environment.

Of course the most obvious effect of this size and type of mass migration into the immediate urban hinterland has been the swallowing up and obliteration of the countryside and of small rural towns and villages. The story of Levittown's displacement of the Long Island potato farmers and their fields is the story of 90 per cent of megalopolitan countryside; the fate of Yonkers and the Tarrytowns is the fate of innumerable older suburbs and towns from Philadelphia to Boston and west to Albany. And not only has the countryside been physically devoured—it has also been psychologically and socially transformed.

The establishment of millions of exurban people in formerly rural areas has both sophisticated and homogenized rural outlooks. In some ways this has been advantageous—the higher standards of medical, educational and municipal services for which urbanites fled in the first place have brought benefits to rural people. It may also be conjectured (with many important reservations) that urban habits of greater toleration for group and personal differences, carried into the countryside, have had some effect in broadening narrow rural beliefs, of liberalizing rural politics and thought. But these advantages have been very limited, both by the fact that when the real-estate developers move in, rural people move out, and by the fact that so much suburban development has taken place in non-inhabited wasteland. Furthermore, suburbs once established tend to be ghettos, insulated from the rural or small town people who happen to be their neighbors. In any event, the social or psychological benefits conferred upon the countryside by suburban development are far outweighed by the homogenizing and deaden-

On the following page:
Dispersal of function; this corporate headquarters in
the New Jersey countryside was formerly located at
56th Street and Fifth Avenue in Manhattan.

ing of taste and opinion throughout the megalopolitan region.

This cultural regimentation is not produced so much by the suburb as *by* the city *for* the suburb. The exurbanites did not leave their tastes, fashions, opinions and life-styles behind in the city. As their numbers reached the millions, it became increasingly profitable for the city to continue to cater to them at long distance. Thus the proliferation of branches of Manhattan department stores and even specialty shops many many miles from the parent institutions; thus the establishment of complex distribution systems to flood shopping centers and supermarkets with the same products offered for sale in the city (and thus the destruction of regional specialty cooking, for example). Rural and small town inhabitants of megalopolis, as a by-product of the city's pursuit of the exurban market, have become all but indistinguishable in taste, opinion and outlook from either suburbanites or city dwellers. And of course the means of mass communication, especially television and national magazines, city centered and city oriented, with a vast exurban audience now in the countryside as a base, have completely smothered local entertainment and cultural activities.

It may be objected that the emphasis placed on the suburban displacement of the countryside, both physically and culturally overlooks the establishment and preservation and improvement of truly vast areas of megalopolis as public parkland. But public parks are not what is meant by "countryside." Most of the parkland in megalopolis is federal national preserve land; it was chosen on the basis of its own needs (for example, as a wildlife sanctuary or forest) and not because of its situation in relation to city, town or suburb. Access to this parkland has been provided almost solely by highways—highways extending not just to cities but to vast suburban districts, so that on weekends or during vacation time, the parkland is so crowded as to provide but little relief from the normal congestion visitors live with daily. Finally, it may be pointed out that public parkland, even though it is left in its "wild" or natural state, is a formal approach to countryside organization. These parks are for recreation *only*, and while admirable for that purpose, they do not provide the variety in countryside that is one of its essences: wild areas, farmlands of various kinds, very small hamlets and villages, and so forth. It is this natural countryside that has vanished in megalopolis through both urban and suburban spread. But the existence of natural countryside is what provides a "boundary" to urban or suburban development; its disappearance, then (and the failure to replace it with "green belts"), is simply another symptom of exploitative, planless land use.

The scattering of industrial, distributive and managerial facilities from both the city and from older nineteenth-century concentrations has had an increasingly disastrous effect upon suburbia. What can happen when an industry establishes itself on the edge of a settled suburban community has been shown in the case of the Tarrytowns. Equally bad though less obvious effects have resulted from the establishment of industry in what was formerly wasteland or open countryside. Ironically, these bad effects are an inevi-

Island Beach State Park

table product of the attempt by industry itself to rationalize its surroundings. For example, let us say that a large printing company (printing is one of New York City's prime industries), desiring to benefit from lower tax rates, less congestion in freight transportation, and pleasanter surroundings for management and workers, decides to move from the city. Under enlightened management the company decides *not* to blight a suburban area, but to establish itself in open countryside. Architects and landscape engineers are called in. Taking advantage of the fact that space is available, they design an attractively modern one-story plant set in parkland. Single-story construction means that the plant will cover a much larger area, but building costs will be lower, the manufacturing process itself will be more rational and, in any event, space out in the countryside is what is cheapest.

There are, of course, a certain number of workers who will not follow the plant out of the city. But most will—indeed, since their skills are not generally available outside the city, the company will *have* to locate in an area with easy accessibility. Under our system of mono-transportation, that means it must be near main expressways or it must construct new access roads to main motor routes. It must be remembered that many of the plant's workers (especially its management) will not be commuting to it from the city but from suburban areas around the city to which they had long since fled. Since the plant is the only employment establishment in its immediate vicinity, commuting workers will not be able to form car pools (unless by chance a group of them lived in the same area of city or suburb). If five hundred men are employed at this plant, then five hundred cars will descend upon it and leave it all at the same time. A vast parking lot must be provided for them. Furthermore, these cars will no longer be following the established routes from suburb to city, nor even from suburb to suburb; they will be increasing the traffic load on cross routes which must then be improved or expanded.

The semi-isolated plant inevitably attracts to it small establishments such as restaurants and drugstores, to cater to its employees. Thus either begins strip development or the nucleus of a new commercial district. In fact the plant will encourage its employees to relocate within its immediate vicinity—and real-estate and building speculators will not fail to rush in to provide housing. Within a short space of time, sub-suburban development has taken place. If it is successful (measured by efficiency), then other plants will be attracted to the area. More and more of the open countryside that was originally sought is built upon and a community emerges which is not a community. It is simply a diffusion of industry and housing to add to the formless spread of formerly urban tissue throughout the megalopolitan region, to the detriment not only of ex-countryside but also of earlier suburbs increasingly enmeshed in undifferentiated industrial, transportation and housing development districts which re-create the noise, congestion and pollution suburbanites thought they had left behind in the city.

Within the past few years the city has thrown off an entirely new kind of structure into the suburbs—the high-rise dwelling unit set in landscaped parkland. In other words, new waves of suburbanites may not be impelled out of the city in search of their own homes and a private parcel of land; they may seek to live in apartments and a building indistinguishable, except for its immediate outside environment, from the apartments and buildings they have left behind. A good example of this newer suburban development is provided by high-rise building clusters sprouting on the New Jersey shore of the Hudson River near New York City. These building developments cannot be said to be an extension of the city itself; they are too far from it for that, both in travel time and conception. They cannot be said to be the beginnings of new cities; their locations are not suitable for city development. By such measures as employment and commutation they are definitely suburban developments, yet by any measure of what has been most desirable in suburbia (privacy, open housing, personal homeownership, the relaxation of the tensions of "cave dwelling") they are not. Perhaps we can discover what they are by examining one of them.

Opposite Manhattan, rising above the Jersey cliffs, is a tall, round apartment house named by its builders "Stonehenge." In itself an attractive structure, it towers above its immediate environment (a small park, the decaying housing of the town of West New York) to afford magnificent views of the city across the river. Apartments vary in size from two-room to eight-room units—all fairly expensive. The building boasts a swimming pool, a sun deck on the roof, a restaurant and several other facilities as well as ample garage space. Being so close to New York it does not, of course, escape the dreadful smog which envelops that city. But since it is separated from it by a broad river (unfortunately polluted and, at this point in its course, lined with rotting piers) and since access to New York City is by way of narrow old roads to either the George Washington Bridge or the Hudson River tunnels (all incredibly crowded at rush hours), thereby making the journey an hour-long affair, it cannot be said to be part of the city itself. Yet it is definitely an urban, not a suburban, structure.

What "Stonehenge" and other such structures are, in fact, are tiny bits of the city that cannot, for reasons of congestion, zoning and cost, be constructed within the city itself and have therefore arisen at some distance from it. One of the solutions offered to urban congestion in the past was the construction of very high-rise apartment houses which, because they could accommodate more people vertically, could save land in their immediate vicinity, this land to be turned into a park for the inhabitants of the building. Thus one of the city's most pressing problems, the provision of more open space for parks, playgrounds and gardens, would be solved. Without discussing whether or not this is a desirable means of urban reconstruction, one can point out that its development in open countryside is, to say the least, anachronistic—except for the sad fact that open countryside has so vanished within commuting distance of the city that vertical construction in order to provide open space has now, in many areas, become a necessity. The time is foreseeable when suburbia will not be composed of residential areas (whether rich or poor, well- or ill-designed) of

houses, but will consist of giant apartment houses, each surrounded by a small, jealously defended bit of park or garden which is but a faint memory of that countryside suburbanites set out to find.

This brief examination of the mutual impacts and rebounds of city and suburb within the megalopolitan framework might well raise the question: Why does anyone want to live in a suburb—why not live in the city itself since the entire region is turning into a formless, nondefined urban area anyhow? Suburbanites answer by simply saying they prefer the "way of life" available to them beyond the city limits. Therefore it is not inappropriate to examine that way of life in some detail. It may be that it will even afford some clues as to why, basically, megalopolis itself has come into being.

7 A Suburban Life

*The first thing that strikes observation is an uncountable
number of men, all equal and alike.... Each of them
living apart, is a stranger to the fate of all the rest—
his children and his private friends constitute to him
the whole of mankind; as for the rest of his fellow-citizens,
he is close to them, but he sees them not; he touches
them, but he feels them not; he exists, but in himself and
for himself alone; and if his kindred still remain to him,
he may be said at any rate to have lost his country.*

—ALEXIS DE TOCQUEVILLE

The author of *Democracy in America*, writing more
than a century ago, thus foresaw the temper of megalopolitan man with remarkable accuracy; for the
central factor of life in an undifferentiated, formless
environment is estrangement. As civic forms atomize,
so their basic components, human beings, also atomize. But before attempting to demonstrate this, it
would be well to examine the traditional standards of
life, both urban and rural, from which, it is held, suburban or megalopolitan patterns have retreated.

The city has, ideally, been considered the highest
expression of any given civilization. It is not necessary
to debate the city's origins (which some hold to be
basically religious) to agree on this. Egyptian Mem-

phis, Babylon, Ur of the Chaldees, Knossos, Athens, Rome, London, Paris, New York—each in succession (and many others besides) have been the supreme expressions of an entire civilization. Within cities are concentrated the highest expressions of art and culture (necessarily since the city provides the largest market for them); within cities are concentrated the most complex and centrally vital economic controls of vast regions (necessarily since to be effective such controls must be in close proximity to each other); within cities are concentrated the essential political power and social levers of manipulation of great numbers of people living far beyond the urban core (necessarily since the very numbers of city population give it predominant political weight while the concentration of economic power and military strength provide it with the means of domination). When cities have succumbed to rural assault, it has generally been because the entire civilization expressed by the city has rotted from within.

To live in the city, then, is to be surrounded constantly by the signs and symbols of power—whether such symbols take the shape of giant monuments to the gods and mighty temples for their worship, or palaces of kings, or the imitation palaces in which democratic governments house themselves, or great stock exchanges and towers of trade symbolizing an economic power basic to political power. To live in the city is to be surrounded constantly also by the artifacts and accomplishments of man—from paintings to sewers, from symphony orchestras to railroad terminals, from huge libraries to complex commercial and financial establishments. It is, above all, to live in very close proximity to huge numbers of fellow human beings.

The dynamism of urban life grows from the constant tensions and frictions produced by the meetings and interpenetrations of so many people and institutions. That dynamism encourages material "progress," and, more importantly, encourages human progress in such matters as intellectual advance (the city is the memory unit of civilizations), social tolerance, and civic participation. But urban dynamism has also, historically, encouraged unrealistic dreams of and adoration of power for its own sake. The goal of urban life has always been widespread humane civility, its potential disease collective megalomania.

To encourage the former and innoculate against the latter, cities ought to be limited to a human scale. Their citizens ought not to be surrounded by signs and symbols so vast and domineering as to belittle the human spirit and human individuality while exalting abstractions of power. Cities ought to provide an environment conducive to human face-to-face encounters, to the essential *accidental* and informal exchange of views, tastes, dreams, aspirations. Cities ought to provide a stage upon which human beings can enact civic and social roles which encourage them to surmount personal debilities and to experiment with new and perhaps more congenial life-styles. As the repositories of accumulated human knowledge and culture, cities ought to be places which encourage direct individual participation (as opposed to mere onlooking) in learning, art and all the many facets of culture.

It is painfully apparent that no American cities

A quiet place for the old folks—
West New York's Senior Citizens' Park
overlooking New Jersey's Hudson riverfront

today fulfill, even in modest degree, any of the above-mentioned functions. All these possibilities of urban life have been subordinated to the worship and exercise of power—material, economic and political—for its own sake. Life in our cities, irrespective of slums, pollution, smog, congestion or frustration, has therefore become intolerable to significant numbers of people. Those hopelessly trapped within the urban centers chant "Burn, baby, burn!" Those who can, flee to a rural environment.

The rural environment has, ideally, been considered the life-nourishing basis upon which civilization rests. Again and again throughout history, when cities, succumbing to megalomania, have withered or collapsed, the latent forces of the countryside have eventually produced a new civilization and new or reborn cities. Rome, London, Jerusalem and many another city have all at one time or another been reduced to barely village size, only to rise again as new expressions of new civilizations germinated in the rural environment.

In rural surroundings are to be found the basic expressions of biologic life on earth: land, water, sunlight, growing plants, animals, the entire symbiosis of nature. To live in the countryside is to be surrounded by the evidence of nature's delicacy and might, to be constantly reminded not only of man's kinship with every living thing, but also of the fragility of man in an evolutionary scale measured not by centuries or millennia but by millions of years. To live in the countryside is to have the opportunity, through seclusion and insulation from vast numbers of one's fellow men and their works, to shed tensions and compulsions, to develop and express personal maturity and individualism, even eccentricity. The rural environment is the place where, above all, by contemplating one's individual existence against the vivid tapestry of nature, the human being may relate himself in meaningful ways to the universe. Although they have always been formalized in the city, every one of the world's great religions sprang originally from the "wilderness." The goal of rural life has always been individual moral and spiritual nourishment, its potential diseases provincialism and egomania.

To fulfill its functions without provoking its dangers, the rural environment ought to remain as "natural" as possible. But since we must accept man as an expression and agent of nature also, this environment need not and should not (except in areas carefully preserved much as city museums preserve examples of former civilizations irrespective of their artistic merit) consist of undeveloped wilderness impossible of human habitation. A countryside ought to consist of woodlands, waterways and lakes, farms, villages, small towns—an area in which individuals can, if they wish, find solitude or human company; an area in which they can either contemplate nature or wrest a living from it.

It is painfully apparent that within the region of megalopolis what little rural environment that can be said to fulfill the above-mentioned functions is fast disappearing. The refugees from America's antihuman cities have almost no opportunity in the megalopolitan region of finding that rural life-style or those rural values which consciously or subconsciously they seek. What do they find instead?

The definitions of life in suburbia (all of which

must, necessarily, be generalizations against which innumerable personal exceptions may be urged) are, basically, isolation amid multitudes, alienation from nature in a nonurban environment, conformism in (relative) privacy, and *unproductive* tensions. It must be remembered that we are not discussing here an ideal suburban community (of which some very few remain within megalopolis) but of the actual suburban developments which exist and in which the overwhelming majority of suburbanites dwell.

Isolation amid multitudes? The suburban environment is incredibly crowded. Some four million people inhabit the suburban area of Long Island—multitudes indeed. Nor are individual suburbs any longer limited to the 9,000 to 10,000 population level of the older small town railroad suburbs; Levittown's 90,000 people are multitude enough for any rural community. Furthermore, it matters little what the population of any individual suburb may be since they now merge one into another, providing truly staggering population totals for any given region. Yet despite large suburban populations, the structure of suburbia remains scattered, fragmented. Few suburbs have anything remotely like a civic center where suburbanites might meet for civic business or social pleasure. The consolidation of school districts has made schools, which sometimes have served as civic centers, increasingly remote—and, in any case, representative of increasingly less local interests. The concentration of shopping into widely scattered "centers" removes even the potential social intercourse of buying and selling household goods from neighborhoods.

The rural housewife who not so long ago knew and

dealt with her local schoolteachers, her town politicians, her neighborhood butcher, her grocer, her many local tradespeople as individuals, often friends, has been transformed into the suburban housewife who is basically a chauffeur or trucker. The trip to supermarket or shopping center is too far and (on congested roads) too nerve-wracking to make more than once or twice a week. The impersonality, size and semiautomated "self-service" nature of these establishments in any case discourages personal interchange. From being a daily personal situation of individual response to individual, shopping (one of the housewife's prime functions) has been reduced to a mechanical, impersonal chore. As for having personal contact with politicians or civic administrators, in very many cases these simply do not exist, the civic or political framework of the suburb being merely a neighborhood in some other political unit. In any case, once again, impersonality is a function of distance and numbers. The politician who must deal with fifty or one hundred thousand constituents cannot take the time to involve himself in personal meetings or persuasions. The village mayor knew it was good politics to visit and get to know as many of his few thousand constituents as possible; suburban civic functionaries must operate through impersonal mass communications media to make themselves heard today. The same enforced impersonality and lack of contact is to be noted in consolidated schools where teachers deal with classes of forty to fifty pupils and administrators are responsible for the education of thousands of students from widely scattered areas.

It is of course true that suburbanites have families,

neighbors and friends—so do city dwellers. But life in a rural environment used to mean (and ought to still) that one inhabited a community in which, at least potentially, it was possible to know almost everyone else. This was the basis for that friendliness, neighborliness and sense of personal social security which distinguished rural from urban community life. Suburbia offers almost no facilities for accidental encounters or for collective meetings; social participation beyond the narrow range of family and friends is limited to the passive receipt of goods, information or entertainment from impersonal and isolated sources. Nor, it must be remembered, is this social isolation a function of "being alone with nature," or "communing with the wilderness"—both sometimes desirable ends. For the suburbanite does not exist in physical isolation in nature. Beyond his windows or his windshield he can see nothing but miles of houses more or less like his stretching in a web to the horizon. The sense of multitudes is always present—and only increases the sense of social and civic isolation.

Isolation contributes, strangely enough, to conformism in privacy. It will be recalled that one of the main attractions of suburbia, historically, was the fact that there, in a private home set at some distance from other homes, suburbanites would be free to express their fancy, to indulge their eccentricity unmolested by the proximity of hordes of neighbors. Of course the essential ingredient of this recipe was the absence of the hordes. In most suburban developments today this factor is lacking. Still, houses are separate, some land always intervenes between them, there are no people living above or below the inhabitants, there is no landlord to placate (only the mortgage-holding bank which cares naught for eccentricity in one's private life provided the payments are on time).

Yet the very structure of suburban developments fosters conformity, first of all (and primarily) because suburban developments are built entirely for one income level and, broadly speaking, one level of taste. The very fact of moving into a suburban development already defines the suburbanite as someone of a certain level of income (which implies a certain level of education, a certain background) who finds the development and its housing attractive—or at least not so repugnant that he is unwilling to dwell there. An extremely important part of this observation is that not only are richer or poorer people excluded by the very nature of any particular suburb, but people of different color (blacks in the East, blacks and Mexican-Americans in the Far West) are excluded. They are excluded not only because of their entrapment in the vicious circle of dependence on urban relief and employment, but also as a matter of policy by the majority of real-estate speculators who build the suburbs. In this, the speculators are only acceding to the demands of most of their potential clients, who fear that the establishment of nonwhite families in their neighborhoods will lower property values.

So far we have been discussing the external conformism imposed by any given suburb—the uniformity of its houses, streets and inhabitants. But the impulse to conform goes deeper than that. Only in the very richest suburbs is there any sense of real privacy, provided by ample land or clever landscaping around houses; in the overwhelming majority of suburbs the neighbors are ever present just beyond their picture windows. There is (generally) no law or rule that compels a suburbanite to mow his lawn, to paint his house in a color that does not "jar" the general color pattern of the street, to own a car neither much cheaper nor much more expensive than everyone else's, to dress himself and his children in the same style as his neighbors, to subdue any signs of individuality or rebelliousness in his children (even if that is only expressed by long hair). Yet sociological studies confirm that, in the suburbs, the pressure of majority opinion is a much more potent force than the law in pressuring people to conform to majority standards. More idiosyncratic behavior is to be found in the cities than in the suburbs—largely because, ironically, city dwellers enjoy more *actual* privacy (owing to the indifference of their neighbors) than do suburbanites.

But majority opinion and its pressures are not the most potent force toward conformism in the suburb. That force is a function of the suburbanite's isolation— it is the fact of his dependence upon mass communications media for his primary contact with the world of men beyond his circle of friends. Especially in the vast fringe areas of megalopolitan suburbia, the suburbanite's relation to everything beyond his home is prepackaged, predigested and transmitted to reach him privately, not publicly (mostly in the deep privacy of his darkened living room, where he stares at the TV). The information a suburbanite receives (as advertising, news or entertainment) is exactly the same as that received by all his neighbors. Upon this information, or in response to its implied suggestions, he styles his life. It is not surprising, then, that his life-

style is pretty much the same as everyone else's. It may be objected that much the same dependence upon mass communications with their impulse toward conformity exists in the cities. But in the city, people are constantly exposed to a tremendous variey of groups whose response to mass communications, if predictably the same within any given group, differ widely *between* groups. The suburbanite lives entirely within one social stratum. At the same time the city offers (not as much as it should) public meeting places and occasions where the validity of mass communication information may be discussed and, perhaps, rejected. Most suburbs offer neither such places nor such occa-

143   *A Suburban Life*

sions. And even if they did, attendance at any public function would be limited to that single social group which composes any particular suburb.

The suburbanite's alienation from nature is almost as complete as the city dweller's. True, the suburbanite has a bit of land with, perhaps, flowers and trees and bushes upon it; he can see the sky if he looks up; he has greater opportunities to keep household pets. But all of this would be provided in any decent urban environment (public parks and parklets or greens taking the place of individual plots); only the fact that there are few if any decent urban environments in the United States gives the suburbanite a slight edge in being closer to a few aspects of nature. But is this all nature has to afford— a small patch of trimmed lawn bordered by a few flowers and boasting a tree or two? Is this the "natural environment" to which suburbanites supposedly originally fled? If so, they might have done better to pitch a tent in a city park.

Nature is many things—but among them may be included open landscape, wild landscape and an intimacy with such natural processes as life and death. The wild or open landscape, for the suburbanite no less than for the city dweller, can be reached only after a long and exhausting journey by car. As for any intimacy with natural processes, the suburbanite is as cellophaned away from them as the city dweller. Let us take but one example. Man is undeniably a carnivorous animal. That he may flourish, other less fortunate animals must be born, raised, slaughtered and butchered, their remains then distributed to the human animal who will devour them. To many people (perhaps the majority) certain aspects of this process are so distasteful that they prefer not to be aware of them. The lamb or calf browsing in an open field (a sight as remote from suburbanites as from Manhattanites) is pleasant to contemplate. Not so pleasant to contemplate is its birth or its death. Yet both of these are the prime facts not only of the animal's existence but also of man's. To shut these facts from one's mind, to paint them in colors of emotional disguise, is to alienate oneself both from nature and from the essential human condition. Yet the suburbanite, one of whose avowed goals was to "get closer to nature," just like his city cousin, will never get any closer in fact or awareness to these central natural phenomena than the artificially colored, frozen, precellophaned lamb chop he buys at the supermarket.

It is not necessary to live in a slaughterhouse to relate oneself to the natural world. People who live in in the countryside (where that still exists), farmers and small town dwellers in farming districts, are intimately aware through simple proximity of the natural order of birth, life and death. To be unaware of this order has always been one of the losses imposed by urban life; the loss becomes still more debilitating when it is suffered by people who do not even have the compensations unique to urban life to replace it. In fact, in one respect at least, city dwellers may be "closer to nature" than suburbanites; most cities at least have zoos where some animals may actually be seen. Few suburbs, if any, can offer that.

Yet, it is urged that even if insulated from the most vital natural processes and removed in distance from real natural landscape, suburbanites at least lead a "more natural life" than city dwellers. Inevitably what is meant by this statement is that the suburbanite spends more time out-of-doors and has to cope with his immediate environment (the house and patch of ground) himself. One of the joys of suburban life is supposedly "doing it yourself" as a means of relaxation and a return to manual or semiskilled labor, a relief of working with real, solid materials and objects after spending the working day dealing with ghostly objects embodied only on innumerable pieces of paper.

It is definitely true that suburbanites spend more time out-of-doors. Their plot of land invites them to do so, whereas most city dwellers are faced with a longer journey to find a suitable park. Yet one irony of the situation is that city dwellers, if they spend less time out-of-doors, walk more than suburbanites—walking is an important natural function. In very many cases, it is quicker and easier to walk to a destination in the city than to attempt to cope with deteriorated rapid-transit systems or fight one's way through incredibly congested traffic jams. On the other hand, so complete is the suburbanite's dependence upon his car, so great the distances from his house to most central locations, that many suburbs do not even provide sidewalks—it being assumed that everyone will drive wherever they are going. An extreme example of this is the suburb of Bel Air outside Los Angeles—so rare are walkers there that the police stop and question pedestrians as potential criminals, vagrants or otherwise undesirable types.

As far as the do-it-yourself craze is concerned, it is

A vanishing phenomenon—the personally owned vegetable stand selling fresh, not prepackaged, produce

common to both city and suburb equally. Rare is the urban landlord who will undertake any kind of repairs or improvements, and rare is the city dweller who has not done whatever had to be done himself, sooner or later. While the suburbanite, faced with the necessity or opportunity of undertaking large-scale structural changes in his house, may develop greater skills, the city dweller faced with the decay of his apartment may develop greater ingenuity.

One of the most glaring symptoms of a suburban life marked by isolation, alienation, and conformism is the growth of *unproductive* tensions. In the open countryside it may be possible (though this is doubtful) to escape most of the tensions of modern life; in suburbia or the city it is not. Yet some tensions may be productive. The tensions of city dwellers generated by simple proximity to immense masses of people, giant institutions, towering structures, vast accumulations of culture, *may* produce either directly or indirectly (as a means of escaping them) thought, intellectual stimulation, even art. But the tensions of the suburbs, of a very different order, are largely unproductive. First of all, what are they?

For the male inhabitants of suburbia, one of the most important additional tensions is the lengthening of the workday. By whatever amount of time is required for a suburbanite to reach his place of employment (the average is about one hour each way), his workday is lengthened. It is, of course, conceivable that this time spent in traveling might be relaxing or even recreational. But the great majority of suburban commuters do not and cannot find it so. They are condemned to waits on railroad platforms, extremely crowded trains on which they are lucky to find a seat, congested traffic at both ends of their trip—all the noisome fret and strain of depending on a decaying and technologically obsolete public transportation system. Or they are faced with the even grimmer task of driving their own car to work. This entails, inevitably, a dangerous and nerve-tautening trip at high speeds down crowded throughways and expressways, traffic jams and delays at the city's edge, a frustrating search for parking space on arrival or the additional financial strain of garaging their cars.

Transportation provides a fruitful source of tensions to the suburban housewife as well. She is condemned to being a chauffeur or trucker. Very often she must either drive her children to school or to the distant schoolbus stop. She must drive to the shopping center. She must often drive her husband to the train or bus station and then drive to pick him up there at the end of the workday (as she must also drive to bring her children home from school). If the children engage in any group activities outside the school, such as Boy Scouts, they must be driven to meetings. Almost every errand or task that the suburban housewife has to perform involves her use of the family car. Of course, since her journeys are usually local, unless she inhabits a suburb built around an older town, she has few traffic problems to contend with. But the constant dependence upon and employment of the automobile is in itself a producer of tensions.

Furthermore, the suburban wife's tasks are performed largely in isolation. Only by chance may she expect to meet a neighbor while shopping; as for her laundering, house cleaning, cooking, and so on—these

labors, which used to be performed (in rural areas) among groups of friends, are now undertaken with only machines for company. In fact, especially on the edges of mass suburbia, the housewife's life has become singularly disembodied—she communes with gadgets, hears voices from her radio and TV but cannot answer them. This aspect of isolation is also, of course, the lot of her husband during the time he spends at home.

The lack of variety in both the physical and social

surroundings of any given suburb produces a mind-dulling boredom and sense of futile conformity which is also a rich source of tensions, even though these may not be so obvious.

Of course much of what has been said above could be equally said of life in any American city. But the frictions and tensions of modern life, when due to or experienced within a variegated environment, *may* be productive. In the suburbs they are simply nakedly frustrating. Apart from the question of whether or not tensions may be productive, in the city people have opportunities to escape them by immersing themselves ("losing themselves") in the thousand-and-one cultural and recreational facilities available. In a true countryside, modern tensions may be shed by immersion in nature. But in suburbia, very few if any means of escaping tension are offered by the environment. Recreational facilities are few (and involve even more use of the car), cultural facilities are all but nonexistent (with the occasional exception of a public library devoted in any case to the uses of schoolchildren, not adults), and nature lies somewhere beyond a horizon crowded with more suburban development. The truth of these observations is established by the heavy commuting undertaken by suburbanites to reach either the cultural and recreational facilities of the nearest city or the natural environment of the nearest state or national park.

It is doubly ironical that suburbanites, having fled the city because of its tensions, must return to the city to relax; having eschewed the countryside for its isolation, they must seek it out for a bit of peace and solitude.

8 Civic Disintegration or Civic Rebirth?

We Americans have a penchant for believing that sufficient inputs of energy and dollars can solve any problem.
We rush in where angels fear to tread and frequently we profit, but sometimes we learn why the angels, in their greater wisdom, have not joined us and prefer to stay aloft. Urban reconstruction is a case in point.

—ADLAI STEVENSON

Certainly there has been no evidence of angelic participation in the various schemes, experiments and proposals brought forward to reconstruct American urban life and its containers. Had the emerging problems of urban sprawl and indiscriminate pillage of the countryside been faced even thirty years ago, the problems would have at least been within the grasp of man to solve. Perhaps they still are—but they are growing in size and complexity so rapidly that they threaten very soon to escape all rational control.

For example, not so long ago the problem of urban renewal was essentially one which could be attacked on the basis of the needs of a particular city. The problem of conservation of natural resources seemed merely a matter of setting aside, by law, certain areas of the countryside. The problem of transportation was a question of bringing the possibilities of motor transport to bear. But now none of these problems can be solved without solving all the others and many additional problems besides, some of which did not even exist before World War II. So inextricably entwined are the various elements of megalopolis that none can be reformed in isolation.

For example, one of the vital measures that must be taken to rebuild major cities as humane environments is the all but absolute banning of private motorcars from their cores and the elimination of space-devouring expressways from the city scene. But this cannot be realistically attempted so long as millions of suburbanites must depend upon their cars to bring them to work in the city. Likewise, an urgent urban problem is that of relocating industry in such a way that it does not befoul the city environment. But under our present lack of system, this relocation only leads to a befoulment of the suburban or country environment. On a deeper level, city reconstruction, under the present American political system, depends upon federal and state approval, impetus and tax money. But the increasing constituency of state and federal government is the bulk of a suburban population who display little concern about their own civic environment, almost none about the environment of cities in which they may work but do not live. The central problem of megalopolis is the continuing migration of city dwellers escaping a deadly environment and, in their movement, destroying an entire region of the country. These people can only be recalled to an urban environment when that environment becomes livable—but their flight has been one of the major contributions to the decay of cities.

America's large cities have many problems peculiar to themselves but the problem most intimately and importantly linked to the megalopolitan environment is disassociation of function. That is to say, cities have been tossing their functions and institutions farther and farther away from their urban cores out into the surrounding areas. Industry, residence, now even management follows a pattern of flight from the urban container which leaves it increasingly impoverished and polarized. The day can be foreseen when New York will consist only of office buildings, slums and massive hotels built to accommodate the transient rich. All its other functions will be scattered over an area reaching from Boston to Philadelphia, and to make these functions accessible ever more and larger expressways and throughways will spill their concrete over both the rural and urban landscape.

The explosion of the city has also a disastrous effect on its surroundings. There are, for example, a few independent small towns left on the outer fringes of the megalopolitan region. But at the rate that urban commerce is establishing itself in the outer reaches of the region and that urban populations are migrating, these will soon be converted into mass suburbs. The day is clearly in sight when the entire mid-Atlantic seaboard of the United States will be one mass of undifferentiated construction—housing developments, throughways, industrial plants, high-rise suburban structures, shopping centers and strip developments

with only an occasional national or state park to relieve the congested landscape.

And yet the power and technology of megalopolis are potentially capable today, as never before in the past, of providing rational and humane solutions to the area's problems. For example, as we have seen, rapid, comfortable and sane mass public transportation is now technically feasible: land and aerial railway trains traveling at speeds in excess of 150 or 200 miles per hour (silently and comfortably too), speedy and large Hovercraft to make use of the neglected megalopolitan waterway system, new types of airplanes requiring fields no larger than a backyard or a pasture to take off and land, continuous-belt freight transportation systems built underground—all these and many more besides. But no improvement in public transport will do more than exaggerate megalopolitan problems if those improvements are undertaken simply for themselves, without being part of a developmental plan for the entire region, one which embraces cities, towns and countryside in their entirety. Otherwise improved transportation will only encourage a further drift of population and scattering of functions.

This illustration brings us to the central necessity for urban and rural regeneration in the megalopolitan region (and perhaps, all of the United States): regional planning. The problems of megalopolis far transcend the political limits of counties and even of states. In order to cope with them, planning must be on a regional scale—and to be effective, regional planning must be supported by regional political authority. In order to solve their urban problems, in other words,

Americans are called upon to be as inventive as the framers of the United States Constitution and devise new means and areas of political jurisdiction and expression within their federal system. But before considering whether or how such political inventiveness might emerge, it might be best to see what benefits could flow from a regional plan and what its elements might be.

The first and foremost task of megalopolitan planning must be one of definition. Cities, towns and the countryside must be clearly defined and delimited. Urban construction must not be permitted to seep over urban borders; suburban sprawl must not be permitted to engulf towns and villages; open countryside must be preserved as such, not degraded by industrial speculation or strip development. Provision must be made for a wide variety of human uses of the land— farming, industry, state parks, villages, towns, cities, green belts of countryside between them, rights of way for public and private transportation—but these uses must not be permitted to impinge upon each other. In short, *form* must be re-created and then reimposed on the formless mass of megalopolis. What should these forms be?

Perhaps the most urgent and important task confronting regional planners will be the creation of new cities. This is the only possible solution to the problem of providing housing and accessible employment for a fast-growing population and yet preserving significant portions of the land as countryside. When, in ancient Greece, a city surpassed what its citizens considered to be an optimum population level for humane civic life, then the surplus population was siphoned off by the creation of new cities, colonies of the old. This ancient device now beckons megalopolitans. The new cities must be planned and built in their entirety as *cities*—not boom towns which will hopefully coalesce eventually into urban conglomerations. From the very beginning they must be planned to include residential, industrial, commercial, cultural, recreational and civic government facilities. And to attract population both from the overcrowded older cities and the over-crowded suburban sprawl, they must be designed to provide both the essential urban condition of density of population *and* a more humane, relaxed and meaningful way of life than is at present to be found in older cities or in suburbia. None should be built to accommodate less than 100,000 people—none to accommodate more than 150,000 people. Residential density (not counting public space) might perhaps be pegged at one hundred inhabitants per acre, a figure which many urban experts consider optimum for city habitation.

People cannot be simply legislated out of their homes; they must be lured from them. New "garden" cities which express the best that urban life can offer will attract confirmed city dwellers from the devastated older cities; they will also attract suburbanites who live outside the older cities only because they have, in fact, become devastated areas. The removal of significant numbers of inhabitants from such cities as New York, Boston or Philadelphia would in turn give those older centers a chance to redesign and rebuild themselves. Likewise the relief of population levels in suburbia would provide an opportunity to retire mass suburbs back into countryside. Legislation could provide, too, not a goad but an active positive appeal to suburbanites and residents of older cities to move to the new cities in such ways as providing tax relief and other financial inducements to mass employment industries to relocate there. And why not tax inducement to private citizens as well? Why not that good old American tradition of providing the new settlers with a "grub stake," perhaps in the form of free rent for a significant number of years, or perhaps ownership of their apartments conditional upon the monthly payment of very low maintenance charges? If the new American frontier is the urban frontier, then perhaps we can find in our pioneer past and its traditions some of the means to cope with it.

The transportation system, has, of course, to be rationalized. We have already spoken of some of the technical means at hand for reviving mass public transportation. If these are developed successfully and combined with an equally essential reconstruction of city rapid-transit systems, very few people should *want* to drive their cars from countryside to city. But, obviously, provision must be made also for motor transport. Here again, the problem is largely one of differentiation. Wide and speedy throughways are necessary for interstate and interregional private travel. The should be routed *only* for that. They should not be permitted to pass through or even very near small towns, nor should they be permitted to invade cities. Local private auto transportation should be confined, as much as possible, to local roads—and these should be constructed small enough to discourage their use for high-speed through traffic. Roadside catering (service stations, inns, restaurants) should be licensed only for long-distance routes that do not pass close to suitable facilities in towns, and the licensing should be based on maintaining a reasonable distance between facilities and also on their design and architectural merits. Strip developments and roadside advertising, already banned on through routes, should be legislated and zoned out of existence on *all* routes.

The problem of dismantling thousands of suburban dormitory developments is a knotty one. Yet unless that is done, space cannot be gained for the reestablishment of green belts between cities and natural countryside. It is hoped that the new cities will attract very

significant portions of the present suburban population—but there are other means of eliminating or
changing that suburban environment which may remain. First and foremost of these would be the re-
quirement that, just as the new cities must be built
complete as cities, so any community established outside the cities must be established as a full and complete *community*. In other words, if real-estate speculators wish to develop housing, they will also have to
provide local industry, commerce and civic structures
—in short, they will have to build not suburbs, but
small towns. Furthermore, zoning permissions should
be granted for such development only when the new
towns meet strict architectural, design and landscaping
standards that both ensure beneficial, humane living
conditions for the residents of the new town and also
determine what impact the new town will have on
the local countryside around it. The population of any
town, old or new, ought to be limited to not more than
about 10,000 to 12,000 inhabitants in any case. Its
ground size should be limited to the pedestrian scale.
It goes without saying, of course, that both the new
towns and the new cities must be complete civic-
political entities with their own responsible local governments.

But what of some of the older suburbs which may
retain their population? What, for example, could be
done about Levittown if a significant proportion of
Levittowners decided to remain there? First of all, it
could be legislated into a real civic self-governing entity. Secondly, local public transportation might be
provided (speedy electric busses, for example). Third-
ly, as an independent civic entity it might be required

to provide a town center to house its civic administration and service headquarters. The school system could, to a certain extent, be decentralized (especially on the grade-school level) so that schools became again essentially neighborhood centers. With all the technical facilities for instantaneous communication now available, that would not necessarily imply any lowering of scholastic standards. Tax powers might be used to discourage shopping centers and encourage independent local neighborhood shops—land for them and for other of these uses might be gained by the municipality buying up the homes and land of those who move away. The municipality might also encourage (or itself undertake) the building of entertainment and cultural facilities—a theatrical center, a music center, for use not only by local residents, but also, through municipal subsidy, by professional groups. An art center, a museum to which the great museums of the large cities could send traveling exhibitions—the list of possibilities is almost endless of ways in which Levittowners could be encouraged to *participate* in public, cultural and civic life. The problems involved in transforming an older, established suburb into a town, a true community, may be more complex and require more time for their solution than the establishment of entire new towns, but they are far from insoluble. The problem of commuting could be dramatically eased, for example, simply by encouraging the establishment of local light industry and management facilities.

One of the basic ideas behind regional planning is, obviously, the return of land to natural countryside. This must not be confused with the establishment of state parks. These should be preserved, and more should be opened—and rapid *public* transport to them provided. But by reestablishment of the natural countryside is meant not simply the preservation of wilderness, but the reintroduction of farmland, hamlet and forest between (and right up to) city and town boundaries——these are the components of a true green belt. The sprawl of suburbia may be removed by some of the methods listed above—but on cleared land, how to reestablish farming (for example) as an attractive way of life? With modern transport and means of distribution and organization, small farming cannot compete with mass production farming, even though the giant "factory farms" are thousands of miles farther away from their prospective urban customers. True—but there are many products better grown on small farms at close proximity to their markets than on the distant great plains. Man does not live by grain alone; he also eats many a specialty food. In New York City, for example, there exists a remarkably large market for exotic Chinese vegetables—most of which used to be grown on small farms on Long Island—but the suburbanization of that area has pushed the Chinese vegetable farmers to greater and greater and less and less profitable distances from the city. Recent statistical surveys of what farming remains within the megalopolitan area show that it is highly profitable, and indicate that much more of it could profitably be undertaken. But even if it were not profitable—the federal government handsomely subsidizes large-scale western farming; why should not a regional government subsidize small-scale local farming? The rewards to the environment of the region's city and town dwellers would be well worth it.

The Garden State Art Center in New Jersey

We have spoken of the establishment of industry in the new cities and towns and also in the older suburbs which remain (transformed into towns). But it must be understood that the industry referred to is light, nonpolluting, non-noisome industry. Only those industries which do not, in their very nature, befoul or engulf either urban or small town environments should be permitted to establish themselves therein. Other industries (as, for example, the huge chemical industries of New Jersey, the vast industrial complex that presently extends, straggling, down from New York to Philadelphia and beyond) should be both goaded and encouraged to reestablish themselves in industrial parks. These parks must be remote from and screened out of both urban and small town areas and must also be insulated from parkland and natural countryside. But this is feasible based upon the provision of new, rapid means of public transportation, both for workers going to the sites and for freight. Neither industry nor management nor distributive facilities should be permitted to establish themselves anywhere they please; their movement or creation should be permitted only insofar as they conform to the regional plan. Incidentally, all industry that corrupts the natural countryside should be forced to move. The Hudson River's shores should be absolutely cleared and returned to the use of the people who live along them, including the inhabitants of New York City. Likewise the seacoast should be cleansed of industry (shipping and shipbuilding being reserved to special, insulated areas) and made into the natural waterfront of the entire region.

Through all of these suggestions (which are but a

few of the many that could be and are being made by regional planners) the new shape of what was once megalopolis may be dimly visible. It is an area of natural countryside, whose rivers, seashore and mountains are reserved as parkland. It is an area of small towns, each of which, being a true civic entity, has its own character. It is an area of great cities, both new and rebuilt, separated from each other by the definite demarcation of countryside and parkland into wide and quickly accessible green belts. It is an area closely knit together for all its natural country spaciousness by very rapid and rational means of public transportation and communication. It is an area that offers every variety of living condition because variety is preserved and enforced in its use of the regional land. It is an area whose inhabitants are all citizens of local communities, whether large or small; therefore it is an area in which civic participation is encouraged. In place of formless suburban and megalopolitan disintegration, it takes advantage of modern technical achievements and political insights to create a new civic integration on a level higher than any that the world has yet seen.

A beautiful dream? Yes—but the elements necessary for translating it into reality already exist. Whether they will be employed depends very much upon the nature of American civilization today and in the immediate future. It depends, finally, on the basic values Americans translate into man-made environment. Before hazarding predictions regarding the future of suburbia-megalopolis, it might be wise to examine these.

Humane Culture
and the Gods of Power

And this is a city
  In name but in deed
It is a pack of people
  That seek after meed.

And hell without order
  I may it well call
Where every man is for himself
  And no man for all.

—ROBERT CROWLEY

Mr. Crowley, writing about seventeenth century London, might well have penned his verse as a description of megalopolis. Note that his criticism is based not upon the physical structure of the city, but upon its moral structure. For him that city is no city if its citizens seek only after meed (profit); indeed, the death of civic spirit leads to complete civic disorder, equatable with hell. And most American city dwellers, along with most American megalopolitans, are beginning today to realize that their environment is a man-made hell. They must also come to realize that this physical environment is only a faithful expression of their general moral and spiritual (or antispiritual) environment. No important changes may be expected in the one without basic changes in the other. And these changes are now a matter of pure survival.

Cities, like people, have a discernible life cycle, one which reproduces the life cycle of the civilizations of which they are the highest expressions. The conjoining of the religious shrine, temple marketplace and religious-political bureaucracy (with its armed expression in the form of warriors) gave birth to the city as a human form. The capabilities of the city as a machine for the domination and exploitation of less organized areas ensured its further growth. But in history, the increasing giantism and overspecialization of cities, leading to a rigidity in their social forms, eventually brought paralysis both to the cities and to the areas they dominated. Rome, for example, went through the cycle: foundation as a religious-political center, expansion as an economic and military power, paralysis as a gigantic center of bureaucratic control of huge regions of the ancient world—and, finally, disintegration and destruction, followed by a rebirth of the city at a much lower level of its culture and power than it had reached before. The only important change that the twentieth century has wrought in that cycle is that the advent of thermonuclear weapons threatens to eliminate the final stage—rebirth—at any level at all.

The growth of American cities, including the cities of megalopolis, has repeated this pattern, though the forms have changed somewhat. Improvements in technology have permitted the metropolitan domination of vast areas to be carried out through remote control. Political control today takes the form of economic monopoly and social manipulation, carried out by

corporations and political divisions centered in the largest cities. Their means are not only the complete centralization of the economy, with control over industry, finance and commerce centered in the great metropolis, nor simply the increasing centralization of the political structure of society more and more dependent on vast armies of bureaucrats housed and working in a few huge urban areas. The means of metropolitan domination today include the centralization and control of the mass communications that knit hundreds of millions of people inhabiting entire continents into one manipulatable mass. Not only does the city decree by what means men shall live and by what means they shall govern themselves, as did ancient Rome, pharaonic Memphis and imperial London —today the city decrees how people shall dress, what they shall eat, how entertain themselves, what information they shall receive upon which to base judgments, and even how they shall think. The domination of the city is a tremendous force for regimentation and standardization of human life. The proof of this assertion is to be found by any objective study of the American megalopolitan region.

But the mindless expansion-for-the-sake-of-expansion of modern metropolitan complexes has been accompanied by an increasing specialization and rigidity in the social forms necessary to carry this out. Men today earn their bread and receive whatever professional satisfaction they may from the accomplishment of increasingly particular and increasingly ghostly tasks. The early twentieth century nightmare-joke about the industrial worker whose sole function is to tighten a particular bolt on a particular machine as it passes him on the assembly line actually predicted the functions of mid-twentieth-century man enmeshed in the management and control of industry and society in the large city. Furthermore, the industrial and political and communications bureaucrats do not even have the benefit of the physical exercise of tightening that bolt; they are chained to desks and the closest approach they make to reality is through the constant receipt and dispatch of billions of tons of pieces of paper. The pieces of paper themselves are now on the way out, soon to be replaced by electronic memory banks and automatic voice and visual means of command over the longest distances. Millions and millions of people today are engaged in work which produces no result (and hence no satisfaction) immediately visible to them. Their rewards are purely financial, that is to say, completely private, not communal or civic.

And, ironically, these rewards are increasingly unable to purchase any but the tawdriest satisfactions in the shape of mechanical toys, subliterate and personally degrading entertainment and a status which loses all meaning when it is submerged in a socially disintegrated and indifferent community of men. The worship of the most primitive expressions of technological control of the environment, power and speed, has actually lost man his control over that environment. The complexity of metropolitan organization hardens social arteries to the point where social change in our giant urban sprawl becomes all but impossible, except through a return to primitive violence.

MOTEL
RESTAURANT
COCKTAIL
Lounge
LAST MOTEL TO BRIDGE
FREE CO
TO ALL CUS
7 PM

A vivid example of what this may mean in actuality was provided recently by events in Berkeley, California (part of the emerging megalopolitan region of the Pacific Coast). There a group of young people, deciding to put into practice in their immediate environment some of the things which urban planners have long advocated, took over an unused area of wasteland and converted it into a public park. They planted grass and trees, erected sculptures, created imaginative structures for a children's play area and so forth. In doing so they were demonstrating how degraded urban space might be rescued for humane use. They were also engaging in a communal effort to produce a tangible, real result, with its attendant personal rewards for them in the shape not of money but in pride of accomplishment and workmanship and the satisfaction of having worked jointly to improve a bit (however small) of their environment.

Unfortunately, the unused area they chose for their park was owned by the University of California's Berkeley establishment. The university, like all other giant corporate organizations, has its own ends, its own systems of control and its own interests. These did not include the conversion of that particular area into a public park. That area was private property of the university corporation. The corporation could only observe that some of its property had been stolen or "appropriated." It immediately proceeded to reclaim what it owned—by the erection of a steel fence around the area and the dispersal of people found within the park. But in order to accomplish this in the face of public disapproval, the corporation had to call upon the help of the police, both state and local, and that super-police force, the National Guard. These law enforcement agencies fulfilled their functions in the ways that seemed best to them—by beating, shooting and gassing very large numbers of people. The result is, of course, a legacy of bitterness, hatred and further social alienation of those elements of society which came into conflict.

Please observe that none of the participants in this affair were acting in any but automatic ways—the only ways they were capable of acting within our megalopolitan society. Only the young people exercised conscious choice, in their decision to improve the environment and to resist the destruction of that improvement. But faced with the degradation of the urban environment, their reaction to it might almost be called automatic—in any event, it *should be.* It should be a normal human response to chaos and filth to attempt to bring into it order and humane decor. The university corporation, given the values of the society it helps to create, could do no more than demand that its property be returned—again, that was an automatic response. It was also automatic for the corporation to call upon the legally constituted authorities to fulfill their declared social functions by seeing to it that the property was returned to its rightful ownership. The police and National Guard were automatically exercising *their* functions when they cleared the park; if they exercised them with unnecessary brutality and more than a little hysteria perhaps that was because they subconsciously realized that theirs was an insane action (though no less insane than that of the university corporation). Insane? Yes—because both corporation and police were engaged in the punishment of a group of citizens whose crime (and legally it was a crime) consisted of an attempt on their part to improve everyone's immediate environment.

For our purposes it is the *rigidity* of the pattern of these events that must be emphasized. A society that can only respond to change in these ways is a society ripe for either revolution or suicide. And the social ossification implicit in the events within the Pacific megalopolitan area is institutionalized throughout the entire urban structure of American life.

We can say then, finally, that we have found suburbia. Physically it is the housing provided for people inhabiting the fast-spreading megalopolitan areas of our country. But more importantly it is a state of mind, compounded of demoralization, fear, the numbing of intellectual faculties and the self-loathing that accompanies a dim awareness of all this. The fear is based on the atomization of life in megalopolis, where every man is isolated from meaningful civic contact with his fellows, where his helplessness as an individual surrounded by the signs and symbols of mighty power and vast masses is constantly impressed upon him. The numbing of intellectual faculties is accomplished by the substitution of lowest-common-denominator mass communications for direct human intercourse. The demoralization is expressed in the suburbanite's flight from social and civic responsibility to a child-and-personal-pleasure environment narrowed to the walls of his own home. The self-loathing is based upon not only his subconscious knowledge of his increasing impotence in an automated, undifferentiated mass hive, but also, perhaps, on his painful awareness that as an American and as a human being he has suffered a massive defeat.

For if the goals of any society, and especially the consciously constructed American society, include the promotion of human happiness, increasing human liberty and the development of the potential faculties within the mind and soul of man, then the establishment of megalopolis must be considered a total defeat for our society. In megalopolis we have produced an environment completely contrary to the expressed aims of the American experiment.

A total defeat, yes—but is this defeat final? If it is, if megalopolis defines the condition of American life for the future, then we can look forward to the completion of the historic cycle of urban development—disintegration and eventual destruction of its present structure. Unfortunately the means available for this demolition have now surpassed all bounds of sanity. If they are employed, not just cities but entire civilizations, perhaps life itself, will be expunged from the planet.

But what if the defeat is not final? Americans have lost a battle—but perhaps they have not yet lost the war. Perhaps it is not too late for reason to permeate the corporate-political structure of megalopolis. Perhaps disgust at the environment and quality of megalopolitan life will prompt new assessments, inspire new civic commitments among us. And if such a general rebirth of civic spirit does not take place, there are always the possibilities of revolution, embodied now in those classes who suffer most from the rigid megalopolitan organization: blacks, the impoverished,

The Statue of Liberty, from New Jersey

the increasing number of people who cannot find niches within the ossified urban machine. And to these may be added the vital leavening of increasing numbers of students and intellectuals who refuse to accept megalopolis and its political and social forms as the final solution to the human problem. The human spirit has a way of reasserting itself when its future looks darkest; in spite of the odds apparently against it, the human revolution against a machine-hive society may well take the place of worldwide holocaust as the means of bringing the megalopolitan nightmare to an end.

In any event we are ready to hazard an opinion—megalopolis is doomed. It will not continue to expand, it will not even continue to exist. Its existence is incompatible with human life and will therefore be terminated in the interests of human survival. Possibly by the conflagration of war—but more hopefully through either a revolution in mass consciousness or a revolution in the political and economic structure and basis of society. In any case, within a clearly foreseeable future one can bid good-by to megalopolis and to the suburbia which is but one of its symptoms.

Index